How to patent an Idea in US

From idea to granted Patent in quickest time, saving costs and making money with your patented invention

by

Prasad Karhad

Copyright © 2018 Prasad Karhad
All rights reserved.
ISBN: 978-1-7200675-9-7

© all rights including copyrights and rights of translation etc. reserved and vested with Prasad Karhad the author. No part of this Book may be reproduced or transmitted in any form or by any means, electronic or mechanical, including photocopying, recording or by any information storage and retrieval system, without written permission from the author.

The information contained within this Book is strictly for educational purposes. If you wish to apply ideas contained in this Book, you are taking full responsibility for your actions.

The author has made every effort to ensure the accuracy of the information within this book was correct at time of publication. The author does not assume and hereby disclaims any liability to any party for any loss, damage, or disruption caused by errors or omissions, whether such errors or omissions result from accident, negligence, or any other cause. While we try to keep the information up-to-date and correct, there are no representations or warranties, express or implied, about the completeness, accuracy, reliability, suitability or availability with respect to the information, products, services, or related graphics contained in this Book for any purpose.

http://patentattorneyworldwide.com/us/

Contents

Contents iii
Introduction 5
1. Patent basics, procedure and costs 13
   How much money can I make by patenting my invention? 16
   Do I really need a Patent ? is it worth the investment ? 17
   Advantages of having patent for your invention: 22
   What can be patented? 25
   Patentability requirements of an invention: 25
   When an idea is patentable? 28
   Inventions not patentable 30
   Who can apply for patent in US? 31
   Short overview of Steps and procedure 32
   Step 1: Idea incubation phase 33
   Step 2: Patentability search (optional step) 35
   Step 3: Patent drafting / writing 37
   Step 4: Filing patent application 39
   Step 5: Publication of application 41
   Step 6: Examination 42
   Step 7: Response to objections 44
   Step 8: Grant of patent / Notice of Allowance 45
2. Idea incubation phase 49
   Get clarity on Idea 51
   Preliminary search 53
   How to search 56
   How to review results of preliminary search 57
   Invention disclosure 61
   How this will save time and costs 63
   Your patent attorney would appreciate this 63
   Mistakes to avoid in idea incubation phase 64
3. Working with a patent agent or attorney 65
   Do I really need patent agent or patent attorney ? 66
   Can I do it myself without Patent practitioner ? 68
   Common mistake if you are do it yourself 69
   Writing patent application is a specialized skill 70
   advantages of going with patent agent or attorney 71
   The responsibilities of patent agent / attorney 73
   First meeting with patent attorney 74

Drafting the first claim in the meeting itself..........77
Patentability search or Novelty search..........78
Opinion on patentability..........79
Advantages of patentability search..........80
Preparing Patent application (patent drafting)..........81
Patent drafting how Patent practitioner does it..........83
Important things about claims:..........83
Important things about drawings:..........85
How patent attorney works on your invention..........87
Proactively speeding up the process..........88

4. Filing Patent application..........89
Patent filing..........90
Types of patent applications..........90
Provisional patent application..........92
Advantages of Provisional patent application..........94
Mistakes to avoid in Provisional Application..........96
Non provisional patent application..........97
Patent co-operation treaty (PCT)..........99
The PCT procedure includes:..........101
Advantages of PCT over convention application..........102
Fees for PCT application..........103

5. After Grant of patent and proceedings..........105
Rights of a patentee..........106
Patent Infringement..........107
strategies to monetize your patent..........110

6. What how why when: Answers to important questions..........113
What is cost of getting patent in US ?..........114
How to hire right patent attorney in US : steps and selection criteria's....120
Shall I go for most expensive patent attorney or most economic one? 122
How much time required ?..........124
When is the right time to file a patent application..........126
Patent Pending or Patent applied status and its advantages..........126
I am in research and development how patent relevant for me?..........127
Not patentable? Here is another option for protection..........129
advantages of using trade secret..........130
Combining trademark and trade secret protection..........132
Choosing between trade secret and patents..........136

7. Important tables charts and references..........139

Introduction

Dear reader,

This book is most valuable for business owners, entrepreneurs, research and development professionals and working employees who continuously come up with
- Innovative ideas,
- new ways to solve a problem,
- do research in specific domain,
- new improvements in existing systems,
- to make system more efficient, or
- new and improved way to serve clients

We will start our journey by **defining our end result** that we want to achieve. The outcome expected from Patent protection is,

"We want our innovative ideas and inventions to have **broadest possible protection**, such that our competitors should not be able to work around our invention without infringing on our patent.

We could have complete monopoly over the patented invention in the market and we would be able to monetize this by working on our invention, licensing it to other company to get royalty payments or completely by selling the patent rights to other business and get significant monetary benefits for your efforts."

The outcome expected from Patent protection

✓ Provide broadest possible protection to our invention
✓ Competitors should not be able to copy or compete with our invention without our consent
✓ Competitors should not be able to work around our patented invention and build similar solution without infringing on our patent (this is most important expectation)
✓ we should be able to monetize the patented invention by
  o by producing patented invention without worrying about competition
  o by licensing it to other company to get royalty payments
  o by completely selling the patent rights to other business and get significant monetary benefits for your efforts

illustration 1.1

You may be:

an entrepreneur or a business owner	with an idea or product to patent
a research scientist	with a new concept, formula to patent
A Professional or an employee	with new idea for software or ecommerce business
a Masters or PHD professional	With your research project to be patented
or a student	willing to learn more about patents

Irrespective of your professional background and field of the invention, the outcome expected from a patent remains the same, "obtaining broadest possible protection to our innovative ideas and making money with your patented invention."

Before we start proceeding, I would like to mention that we are taking a different approach to this important information.

we would be deliberately staying away from the usual educational stuff about intellectual property and patenting invention that is easily available to you. Instead we would be taking **more practical approach**, sometimes may be in an unorganized manner yet effective in bringing the value to you.

As this book and information series is designed especially considering the **your side** (inventor's side) for entire life cycle of the invention and Patent. So, all the while we proceed through this information our focus remains on getting the final outcome (refer illustration 1.1) for your invention.

this book is arranged in

- step by step
- outcome oriented information blocks
- checklists
- and in the workbook format

Where it is specifically designed to guide you through the complicated steps in simple and easy to understand manner to get the best possible outcome with your invention every single time !!!

objective of this book

Most important objective of this book would be **installing a software in your brain** about the wisdom about patents and building right mindset; a software that will continuously help you in:
- spotting the opportunities to secure patents for your innovative ideas
- identifying the innovative ideas at inception level
- taking informed and speedy actions to take that idea to a complete invention disclosure
- moving ahead to a patent filed stage for the invention in shorted possible time
- saving costs and time along the way by minimizing mistakes
- ultimately getting paid for the patented invention utilizing strategies to monetize it

http://patentattorneyworldwide.com/us/

The outline of book

Patent basics, procedure and costs

- Definition of patent and invention, what can we learn from it
- How much money can I make by patenting my invention?
- Do I really need a patent? is it worth the investment?
  or I should use same money elsewhere (to grow business)
- What inventions are patentable
- What inventions cannot be patented
- Short overview of steps and procedure for filing patent
- Costs involved at each stage
- What would be my contribution at each stage as Inventor

Idea Incubation Phase

- How to identify innovative ideas with potential to win patent
- How to do a preliminary search for your innovative idea
- How to review the results you got from this preliminary search
- when to get encouraged and when to get discouraged for going ahead for patent filing based on results
- Creating Final Draft of working invention disclosure
- Mistakes to avoid in Idea incubation phase
- Action items, checklist, worksheet for Idea incubation phase that will help you to create your complete invention disclosure.

Save time, costs while working with a patent agent or attorney:

- Do I really need patent agent or patent attorney?
- Can I do it myself, without patent practitioner
- Common mistakes to avoid
- How the Idea incubation phase, if done correctly is really helpful here
- Effective first call or email with a patent agent or attorney firm
- how to Proactively speed up the patenting process
- how to be ready with expected information at appropriate stages
- Opinion about patentability
- Making decision to go ahead with patent filing based on results
- Preparing Patent application (Patent drafting)
- Important rules for patent claims, detailed description, drawings, references, title, Abstract etc.
- Covering all possible embodiments
- How to ensure that the patent application is written to provide **broadest possible protection** for your innovative idea

http://patentattorneyworldwide.com/us/

Filing Patent application:

- Different options, paths and strategies for Filing patent application
- Provisional patent application
- When to go for provisional patent application
- advantages
- mistakes to avoid
- Non provisional (Complete) patent application
- International patent application
- different options and routes available
- strategies to go about international patent filing
- Patent Cooperation Treaty (PCT) application
- Advantages of PCT over convention application
- Fees for PCT application

Grant of patent and proceedings

- Grant of patent
- Patent infringement
- What rights you can practice on grant of patent
- Different strategies to monetize your patent

What how why when: Answers to important questions

- Cost of getting patent in US (a short note)
- How to hire right patent attorney in US: steps and selection criteria's
- Most expensive v/s most economic patent practitioner
- How much time required ?
- When is the right time to file a patent application
- Patent Pending status and its advantages
- I am in research and development is patent relevant for me?
- Not patentable? Here is another option for protection
- Advantages of trade secret
- Combining trademark and trade secret protection

1. Patent basics, procedure and costs

Patent basics, procedure and costs

- Definition of patent and invention, what can we learn from it
- How much money can I make by patenting my invention?
- Do I really need a patent? is it worth the investment?
  or I should use same money elsewhere (to grow business)
- What inventions are patentable
- What inventions cannot be patented
- Short overview of steps and procedure for filing patent
- Costs involved at each stage
- What would be my contribution at each stage as Inventor

We will start with how patent law defines a patent.

Definition: what is patent?

A patent for an invention is the grant of a property right to the inventor, issued by the United States Patent and Trademark Office. Generally, the term of a new patent is 20 years from the date on which the application for the patent was filed in the United States.

The right conferred by the patent grant is, "**the right to exclude others** from making, using, offering for sale, or selling" the invention in the United States or "importing" the invention into the United States.

Having a granted patent in US for your invention gives you right to exclude others from

- making,
- using,
- offering for sale,
- selling" the invention in the United States
- "importing" the invention into the United States

This implies, when you get patent for your invention, you may able to get significant monetary benefits for your patented invention by:

1. licensing your patented invention to other business and **earn royalties** on regular basis as per agreement
2. you can build a business around your patented invention and stop others from copying it, so there would be no one competing with you with similar product or service, and hence can earn **significant profits**.
3. having patent for your invention may also help in **raising capital** for business
4. You transfer all rights of patented invention to other business. That is make significant money by **selling your patented invention**.

There are three types of patents:

- **Utility patents** may be granted to anyone who invents or discovers any new and useful process, machine, article of manufacture, or composition of matter, or any new and useful improvement thereof;
- **Design patents** may be granted to anyone who invents a new, original, and ornamental design for an article of manufacture; and
- **Plant patents** may be granted to anyone who invents or discovers and asexually reproduces any distinct and new variety of plant.

Note: For the purpose of this book we are focused on utility patents, so whenever we mention a word "patent" in this book hereafter which should inherently mean " Utility patent ", If not explicitly stated otherwise.

How much money can I make by patenting my invention?

This is the most important question each inventor or researcher has in mind when deciding about going for patent, after all monetizing research and development efforts and enjoying monopoly in return of disclosing the invention to the public is the base of patent system.

"The patents are as valuable as they are worth in commercial use."

In other words, there has to be a commercial value for the invention that you are patenting, there need to be companies, businesses who would potentially want to use your invention and paying you royalties. Or companies who could be interested in buying out your patent if you are willing to sale it.

If this part is missing, that is your invention is does not have any commercial value then probably your patent for that invention would also be worthless.

Now, the obvious question in your mind would be...

How would I know the commercial worth of my innovative idea... that has not yet patented?

This question in well answered in a section of this book on provisional patent application and testing commercial worth of the invention refer to chapter "Filing patent application"

The amount of money to be made by patenting your invention completely depends on how much commercially valuable your invention is, and your ability to commercially exploit your patented invention.

For more strategies on making money with patent refer chapter "after grant of patent and proceedings"

Now, let's go to the core question you might have in your mind...

http://patentattorneyworldwide.com/us/

Do I really need a Patent ? is it worth the investment ?

Well, you think about it all the time, when you are in deciding phase:

- is patent really for me?
- is it really worth the investment?
- what if I don't go for patent and **use that money somewhere else** or in growing my business ?

Fair question, the basic reason behind asking this question is whether you will be able to get the return on investment that you are considering to do for patenting your invention. Now, to answer this in most simplest possible way, let's take an example.

Lets imagine a scenario; you are a business owner or a professional and you are continuously being challenged with different problems in your business on daily basis,

one or the other way continuously challenged
to solve problems

while doing that you happened to come up with an innovative solution for your business

And let's assume **your solution** has real commercial potential in **industry**

The solution has a commercial value in the market. let's go fast forward and your company is successful because you have implemented that solution in your business and you are enjoying the success of that particular solution.

your competitors **jump in...**

Now, the competitors will jump in and they are there to compete with you. so they will take your product for your innovative solution what you have designed they will **reverse engineer it** and then they will:

- try to beat you on prices
- will try to beat you on quality may be telling a low quality product at cheaper price and
- they probably will try to beat you on scale production

competitors would do whatever things possible to compete and capture your market share. And ultimately even though you are the inventor you are the creator of that solution; you are the person who first made that innovative idea and worked on it and bring that solution to life, still you end up on losing side.

all efforts that you took goes waste...

we have seen this happening to business around us, as they came up with some new strategy, innovative ways to do something and every competitor copy that and start competing with them and the progress made again comes back to square one.

All the competitive advantage and potential of making significant profits with your innovative idea goes waste. And you don't have any option but to give in to ever growing competition.

Compare this situation with another situation where you have filed a patent application for innovative idea and you got patent granted for it.

Now the situation is different, the competition cannot directly compete with you as patent gives you exclusive rights. "the right to exclude others from making, using, selling, importing or offering for sale your patented invention without your permission" in this case, you yourself can calculate the **return on investment** for your invention.

It is most likely going to be very high potential of profits with your investment in going for patent for your innovative idea, **provided your invention has commercial potential** and you as an inventor or the owner of the invention has the ability and skills required to commercialize the patented invention, and in process make significant money for your research and development efforts.

Another example to illustrate this,

Do you know age of empires ? a mythological game ?

what will happen if a player or kingdom only focuses on financial growth of country and completely ignoring building walls castles and army... ever made that mistake while playing? soon you would be attacked by nearby kingdoms and their army would destroy you. And there is a lesson to be learned from it.

Of course making financial progress and business growth, bringing new clients and more profits is important. However, it is more important **to protect your business** with intellectual properties like patents, trademarks, copyrights, trade secrets etc... which ultimately would be protecting your future profits from the ever growing competition !!!

Not protecting intellectual property of your business would be like building a rich, prosperous country without a defense mechanism or army. It will always be under treat of invasion by other countries (competitors).

Now, all of these examples we have seen from a business owners or entrepreneurs perspective however the inherent advantages and benefits of having a patent for your invention stays the same even though you are a student, working professional or employee or research and development person.

Conclusion:
whether to go for patent or not is a decision that should be based on facts and not to be decided on opinions or misbeliefs. Most important deciding factor would be the commercial potential of your invention.

Let's consider the advantages of getting patent protection for your invention.

Advantages of having patent for your invention:

Owning an intellectual property has some similarities with owning any other form of tangible property like a real estate. So, what are the advantages of having a real estate property on your name?

- You can rent it
- You can sell it
- You can stop others from using it without your permission
- You can use it for your purpose (business or residence)

on similar terms, patent is an intellectual property and has all the advantages stated above, but you need to claim it to be on your name, hence it is important to file of patent application for your invention. and there is a difference though, unlike real estate the patent has the term of 20 years of ownership.

Advantages of owning patent would be:

- You own exclusive rights for patented invention for given time (20 years from filing of patent application)
- You can use it to build a business around patented invention and not worry about competition
- You can rent it (in this case license the patented invention) to existing businesses
- Exclude others for using, selling, offering for sale and importing your patented invention in US
- You can completely sell the patent to other company

hence this gives a unique advantage to patent owner which can be leveraged for have a complete monopoly and competitive advantage from competition and in certain cases having patent may also help in **raising capital for business** !!!

Imagine what it would be like when:

- You have exclusive rights for your invention (idea, project, product etc.) and you can stop other from using your invention for commercial purpose for 20 years from filing date.
- You can make significant return on your investments that you made for research and development and patenting your invention by ways like
    - licensing your patent to other companies,
    - building business around your invention, or
    - completely selling it to other company.
- You will have better chances of getting funded for your idea, business, product etc. If it is protected by patents, as investors clearly see how they can have monopoly in the market by having patented product for business.
- You and your business are perceived as an expert in the industry when you have patent. This helps in finding great employees, partners, financers and clients too. Ultimately it enhances your market value.

Some people have a mis-belief that, Patents are given to only ground breaking (landmark) and complex invention that changes the world...

Which is not true.

In reality the patents are also **granted to incremental inventions** !!! Inventions that have come up with novel and non obvious solution to existing inventions (patents)

What that means is, most of the part of your solution may be already known to public (that is available in the market, patented or published in journals) but you might have come up with something (Novel, Non obvious and useful) that is not an obvious solution to normal person skilled in that domain and solve a small (but significant) problem in existing solutions. In this such case the inventor still can win patent for his invention if other patentability criteria's are mate by his invention

Many inventors getting discouraged by seeing something similar to their invention in the market, published or known to public... what they fail to realize is they may **still have novelty and Non-obviousness in their invention** although prima facie it looks similar to things already known to public.

Don't get discouraged if you see things already in the market, published or known to public which are somewhat similar to your invention... You still may have something in your invention that can win patent.

This is beautifully explained in chapter "Idea incubation phase".

http://patentattorneyworldwide.com/us/

What can be patented?

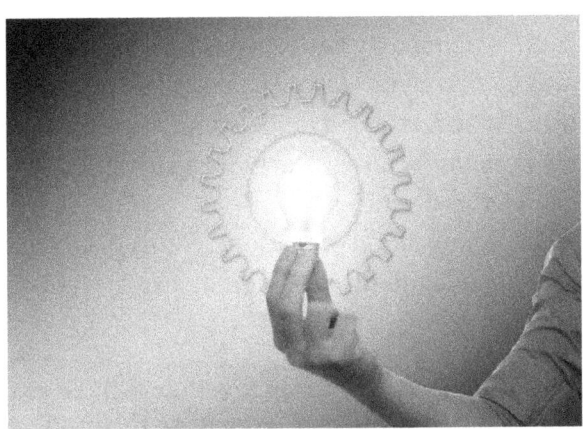

As per §35 U.S.C. 101, patentable subject matter is defined as:

"Whoever invents or discovers any new and useful process, machine, manufacture, or composition of matter, or any new and useful improvement thereof may obtain a patent therefor, subject to the conditions and requirements of this title."

The invention must fall into the category of process, machine, manufacture, or composition of matter. and it should not be falling within an exception recognized by the courts; namely, laws of nature, physical phenomena, and abstract ideas.

Patentability requirements of an invention:

1. The invention should be patentable subject matter, which is any "new and useful" machine, manufacture, process, or composition of matter
2. The invention must be new, or "novel."
3. The invention should be "non-obviousness."

4. The invention must be useful, or offer "utility."

Definitions :

- "process" is defined by law as a process, act, or method, and primarily includes industrial or technical processes.
- The term "machine" used in the statute needs no explanation.
- The term "manufacture" refers to articles that are made, and includes all manufactured articles.
- The term "composition of matter" relates to chemical compositions and may include mixtures of ingredients as well as new chemical compounds.

These classes of subject matter taken together include practically everything that is made by man and the processes for making the products.

Now let's look at each patentability criteria one by one so that we can see if our invention satisfies them and whether we should proceed with filing patent application.

Novelty: An invention is said to be novel if it is not known to public or does not constitute the state of the art.

The invention should not be in publication or being used or known to public or patented in US or other countries prior to filing date. There is 1 year grace period for filing the patent application if the inventor discloses the invention.

Under AIA § 102(b)(1)(A), an inventor has one year from the time he or she discloses an invention within which to file a patent application.

"Non-obvious": This is the most tricky and difficult to overcome requirement for getting patent in US.

35 U.S.C. §103:

"A patent for a claimed invention may not be obtained, notwithstanding that the claimed invention is not identically disclosed as set forth in section 102, if the

differences between the claimed invention and the prior art are such that the claimed invention as a whole would have been obvious before the effective filing date of the claimed invention to a person having ordinary skill in the art to which the claimed invention pertains. Patentability shall not be negated by the manner in which the invention was made."

In other words;

A patent may not be obtained, if the differences between the subject matter sought to be patented and the prior art are such that the subject matter as a whole would have been obvious at the time the invention was made to a person having ordinary skill in the art.

Non obviousness requirement states in order to get patent the invention should not be obvious to a person who is ordinary skilled in the art.

if we review the invention in light of existing knowledge or state of the art, does the invention becomes a obvious next step? If the answer is yes... then the invention is said to be obvious to a person skilled in the art and patent would not be granted such invention. Some of the common things considered as obvious are:

- Combine elements from prior arts the becomes mere combination of prior art elements
- Interchanging or substituting element to obtain similar results
- Use of known technique or methods to enhance invention
  Etc...

In other words, considering the state of the art (things already known to public) and assuming the person skilled in the art does not have any knowledge about our invention, if that person skilled in the art was asked to solve the problem (that our invention solves), then the our invention should not come as a natural suggestion by that person skilled in the art. Which ultimately means invention should not be obvious. This is in essence known as non obviousness test.

And one of the ways that could be helpful in qualifying the non obviousness test of patentability is mentioning and proving to examiner that our invention is

solving a the long standing problem in the industry. Pointing out that the problem existed for long time and there was a need to solve the problem, also mentioning existing prior arts and patent references who tried before but could not solve up to certain extent (stating problems with the prior arts in the background of the invention while drafting patent) and since the problem has not solved till now it ultimately means the solution to the problem that is our invention **was Not obvious**.

Now, this is not your job as an inventor to do all this, in fact this is responsibility of a patent agent or patent attorney working on your invention. an experienced Patent practitioner would be asking you for required details and technicality of your invention and using such information while drafting patent application for your invention which gives a significant chance for your patent application to stand through examination stage till the grant of patent.

This is explained in detail in section "preparing patent application (patent drafting)" under chapter "working with patent agent or attorney"

Utility or useful:

The utility or usefulness criteria of patentability states an invention is "useful" if it provides some identifiable benefit and is capable of use.

When an idea is patentable?

when you are thinking about that innovative idea and its patentability, the first question you need to ask yourself about your idea is how much details you know about that idea... and are these details are enough **to reduce it into practice?**

"innovative ideas (inventions) are patentable only if they are enabling " provided that it satisfies all patentability criteria's.

Your idea would be enabling if the information you have is detailed enough such that a person skilled in art would be able to practice the invention without requiring external help or additional research.

http://patentattorneyworldwide.com/us/

In other words, the information you know about your idea is detailed enough such that a person moderately skilled in the art could practice the invention.

Ideal case would be you actually develop a working model or a prototype of your invention (idea) demonstrating it works, but this is Not always required by USPTO.

When, all you have is 1 line idea about something might work or would work then you should know there is work to be done and efforts to be taken before it could win patent...

That doesn't mean you need to build your invention or a working prototype... all it means is you need enough details about your idea that would help someone to practice it, that is it should be enabling !!!

Inventions not patentable

What is **non** Patentable subject matter in US?

As we have seen in definition of patentable subject matter,

any person who "invents or discovers any new and useful process, machine, manufacture, or composition of matter, or any new and useful improvement thereof, may obtain a patent,"'

These classes of subject matter taken together include practically everything that is made by man and the processes for making the products.

Having said that, there are subject matters which are **non patentable:**

- Inventions related to atomic energy, like utilization of special nuclear material or atomic energy in an atomic weapon, are not patentable as per Atomic Energy Act of 1954.
- As per Interpretations of the statute by the courts
    - the laws of nature,
    - physical phenomena, and
    - abstract ideas are not patentable subject matter.

A patent cannot be obtained upon a mere idea or suggestion. The patent is granted upon the new machine, manufacture, etc.,

Now, this may seem to be going against the vey title of this book "how to patent an Idea in USA".

However, it is talking about **mere idea or abstract idea** which would not be patentable. In fact,

"everything has its beginning in an idea"

Everything begins with an idea, including inventions that win patents. Hence the theme of this book is to help you get from the ideation phase to a comprehensive invention disclosure that you can discuss with your patent attorney as quickly as possible.

and then taking that comprehensive invention disclosure to the subsequent steps like filing patent application, examination, office actions and ultimately to grant of patent for your invention. Helping in saving a lot of time, rework and costs in the process by avoiding some obvious mistakes !!!

Who can apply for patent in US?

An application for a Patent for an invention may be made by any of the following persons:

- The inventor
- inventor's assignee
- Legal representative of inventor or his/her assignee
- If an inventor refuses to apply for a patent or cannot be found, a joint inventor may apply on behalf of the non-signing inventor.

Short overview of Steps and procedure

To understand the steps involved in getting patent for your invention in more clearer way let's assume 3 illustration as below,

1. You (the inventor): who has innovative idea to patent

2. Patent practitioner (Patent agent or attorney)

3. United States Patent and trademark office (USPTO)

We would be seeing what is the **involvement** of each one of them at every step while getting patent. along the way we would also be seeing relevant **costs and time involved** at each stage. So, let's get started...

Step 1: Idea incubation phase

Every invention has its beginning in an Idea. In this phase you capture your idea properly, get clarity on each element of innovative idea, do fill in the blanks with appropriate research and experimentation.

Include drawings, diagrams or sketches explaining working of invention. the drawings and diagrams should be designed so as to explain the working of the invention in better way with visual illustrations. they play an important role in understanding your invention.

Once you have your innovative idea completely captured with all technical details, then you perform **a preliminary search**. This search is for finding answers to questions which builds a working disclosure of the invention.

Some of the questions in invention disclosure form would be:

- What is my idea / invention about? How does it work?
- What problem my innovative idea is solving
- What is the field of my invention
- What are the advantages of my innovative idea
- What are elements or components of my innovative idea
- Can I draw a block diagram or device or flowchart or sketch that explains my invention in better way
- What are advantages of my invention over existing knowledge that is prior arts
- Who are the competitors with what product or service etc..

This is most important phase for inventor where an idea is taken from ideation phase to a working invention disclosure that can be discussed with a patent agent or attorney.

For this important section we have a **complete chapter** about actions to take and worksheets Refer chapter on "Idea incubation phase" in this book

Costs: There are **no costs** involved at idea incubation phase

		Involvement	Responsibilities
Inventor		100 %	Collect relevant details on innovative idea and create comprehensive invention disclosure
Patent agent or attorney		0 %	Receive invention disclosure, perform patentability search, provide opinion and Draft patent application
USPTO		0 %	--

The Outcome of this step:

The outcome of idea incubation phase is creating of working invention disclosure which covers all aspects of your invention completely. And which is ready to be shared with Patent practitioner.

For detailed steps, checklists and guidelines Refer chapter "Idea incubation phase" in this book

http://patentattorneyworldwide.com/us/

Step 2: Patentability search (optional step)

In this step, the patent agent or attorney who is working on your invention helps you in finding out whether your invention meets patentability criteria which are :
- Novelty
- Non-obviousness
- Utility

The patentability search is aimed towards finding out the novelty and non-obviousness of the invention, the search identifies the closest possible prior arts (known to public) relating to your invention and based on the results obtained an opinion about the patentability of your invention may be provided by Patent practitioner.

Based on the results found and reviewed in a patentability search report, the patentability opinion may be positive, negative or neutral. A positive patentability opinion indicates, you stand a good chance to get your patent granted for your invention.

The patentability report and opinion helps you decide whether to go ahead with the patent or not, chances are what you thought as novel might already been patented or know to public in some form of information.

Hence this reports saves lots of time, efforts and cost of the inventor by helping him decide whether to go ahead with the patent filing process or not.

For more details on this important section of patentability search Refer chapter on "working with patent agent or attorney" in this book

Involvement:

You (inventor) 30% involvement about answering to questions by Patent practitioner, reviewing patentability search report and closest possible prior arts.

Patent practitioner 70% involvement: understand invention disclosure and performing patentability search, prepare report and give opinion on patentability

USPTO 0% not involved Yet

Costs: the professional fees for Patent practitioner can range from $500 to $3000

Time : the time required is about 5-7 working days

The outcome of this step:

The outcome of this patentability search report is:
- You get to know about the opinion on patentability of invention
- When we compare our invention with closest possible prior art found in the patentability search report, the non obvious and novel feature would be identified.
- The novel aspect of the invention obtained via patentability search can be leveraged while writing patent application and especially claims of patent such that our patent application stands a good chance going through the examination stage to granted patent.
- In case the patentability opinion is negative, then it saves a lot of cost and time which would be unnecessarily invested in proceeding with patent filing process and eventually getting application rejected.

Note: in spite of all these benefits of the patentability search, this is an optional step. You can choose to directly file the patent application without going for patentability search, which is **Not** recommended by the way.

Step 3: Patent drafting / writing

Patent drafting is the stage where your invention disclosure and patentability search report is used to create the patent application.

Patent drafting / writing is a specialized job, it requires years of practice and experience with patent law to draft a good patent application. Patent is a techno-legal document, technical as well as legal.

You can do it yourself and write patent application for your invention on your own and submitting it to USPTO. But like just like any other complex projects, you would be making some obvious mistakes that a first time patent writer or inventor usually makes, and the list of such mistakes is exhaustive...

Writing patent application is a complex job, there are many rules and care to be taken while drafting claims, writing detailed descriptions, writing different embodiments of the invention, describing inventive step etc...

This is one of the most important step in life cycle of a patent.

"A good patent application written by an experienced patent agent / attorney should adequately cover the scope of your invention and should survive not only through the examination phase till the grant of patent but also it should survive the commercialization phase where actual money is made by licensing or selling patent rights, where competitors should not be able to work around your patent."

Writing such patent application is a skill and that's what explained in detail in our section on "Preparing patent application (patent drafting)" in chapter "working with patent agent or attorney"

Involvement:

You (inventor) 10% involvement about answering questions by Patent practitioner, identifying the inventive step and providing detailed disclosure if required. Review patent application.

Patent practitioner 90% involvement for writing patent application that provides maximum possible protection to invention, following all rules for writing patent application.

USPTO 0% not involved yet

Costs: The cost for drafting a patent application in US varies in a great deal as it is dependent on multiple factors like field of invention and complexity and the cost can range from $2000 to $10000.

drafting Provisional Patent application in US:

Simple invention	Complex invention	Very complex invention
$2000	$3000	$5000

drafting Non-Provisional (complete) Patent application in US:

Simple invention	Complex invention	Very complex invention
$5000	$8000	$10000

Time : it takes about 1 to 2 weeks time for patent attorney to draft an application for an invention. It certainly can take more time based on complexity, length of detailed description and availability of patent attorney's time.

The outcome of this step:
The outcome of this patent drafting stage is :
- A patent application that can be filed at USPTO
- A patent application well written by an experienced patent agent / attorney that survives through the examination phase, till the grant of patent and commercialization phase as well.

Step 4: Filing patent application

Based on the readiness of your invention, the decision has to be made whether to go for provisional patent application or complete patent application. If you are not quite ready with complete invention and requires further research and development yet you don't want to lose on priority date for filing patent application then going for provisional patent application is recommended.

There are some advantages for filing provisional patent application especially in the early state of work on invention which are discussed in detail in a separate chapter about "filing patent application"

Provisional patent application:
- When to go for provisional patent application
- advantages
- costs
- elements of provisional patent application
- mistakes to avoid

The patents are territorial in nature, so if you file patent in US, you are getting protection in US only. You cannot stop use of invention outside US.

Therefore, if you desire that your invention should be protected in multiple countries, depending on your preference of countries different options, paths and strategies for filing patent application is to be adopted with the guidance of patent agent / attorney.

International patent application:
- different options and routes available
- strategies to go about international patent filing
- Patent Cooperation Treaty (PCT) application
- Paris convention and other routes

The details about patent filing is explained in a chapter "filing patent application"

	Involvement:	Responsibilities
Inventor	10 %	reviewing patent application and signing formalities (power of attorney)
Patent agent or attorney	80 %	preparing patent application for filing. recommending best filing route and options for international patent application (if required).
USPTO	10 %	receive patent application and provide the receipt along with date and time of filing the patent application.

Costs: generally there is no professional fees charged for patent filing patent application (provided fees is paid for patentability search and patent drafting)

There are many things needed to consider before giving an exact fees amount, as it depends on number of sheets in patent specification, number of claims etc. but below are approximate costing for this stage.

filing fees for Provisional application in US

Large entity	Small entity	Micro entity
$280	$140	$70

Non provisional Patent application

Basic filing fee - Utility (paper filing also requires non-electronic filing fee under 1.16(t))

Large entity	Small entity	Micro entity
$300	$150	$75

http://patentattorneyworldwide.com/us/

The outcome of this step:

The outcome of this filing patent application is :
- You receive a receipt for filing patent application USPTO with invention title, your name along with time and date of filing.
- Now, your patent application have secured a priority date for your invention, which makes you less worried about confidentiality and safety of your invention.
- The patent application will be taken to subsequent steps requests and fees submitted as per standards.

Step 5: Publication of application

Patent application is published after the expiry of 18 months from the earliest filing date, however if requested by applicant the director may publish the patent application earlier than end of 18 month period.

Involvement:

You (inventor) 0% involvement on automatic publication. or optional step of filing early publication request.

Patent practitioner 10% involvement. optional step of filing early publication request.

USPTO 90% involvement. the patent application is automatically published or if requested early publication is done.

Step 6: Examination

As per 35 U.S.C. 131 Examination of application.

The Director shall cause an examination to be made of the application and the alleged new invention; and if on such examination it appears that the applicant is entitled to a patent under the law, the Director shall issue a patent therefor.

The main conditions precedent to the grant of a patent to an applicant are set forth in 35 U.S.C. 101, 102, 103, and 112.

Once your application has been accepted as complete, it will be assigned for examination. Your examiner will review the contents of the application to determine if the application meets the requirements of 35 U.S.C. 111(a).

The objections raised on your patent application would be communicated with you, by official letter from the USPTO, known as an **Office Action**. You would get opportunity to make amendments or contest the objections raised.

There is specific time within which you will have to respond to the objections, if you failed to do so the patent application will be abandoned.

In the First Action Interview Pilot Program you can have an interview with the examiner. after you have reviewed the objections and results of search conducted by the examiner.

This gives you an opportunity to have one on one discussion with examiner which shortens the time and to and fro communications for resolving objects and it can result in quicker allowance of patent for your invention.

Time:
USPTO takes the application for examination (in about 12-36 months).

http://patentattorneyworldwide.com/us/

Patent Examination Fees

Description	Fee	Small Entity Fee	Micro Entity Fee
Utility Examination Fee	760.00	380.00	190.00

Involvement:

You (inventor) 10% involvement the patent agent or patent attorney makes request for examination on behalf of you.

Patent practitioner 10% involvement request for examination

USPTO 80% involvement. receive request for examination and examiner check patent application for patentability and other criteria and generates search report (office action)

Step 7: Response to objections

Majority of patent applicants (inventors) will receive some type of objections based on examination report. The objections raised on your patent application would be communicated with you, by official letter from the USPTO, known as an **Office Action**. You would get opportunity to make amendments or contest the objections raised.

The best thing to do it analyze the examination report with patent agent / attorney and creating a response to the objections raised in the examination report. This is a chance for an inventor / applicant to communicate his side of the equation and making desired changes in the patent application to comply the objections received.

There is specific time within which you will have to respond to the objections, if you failed to do so the patent application will be abandoned.

If your application is twice rejected, you may appeal the examiner's decision to the Patent Trial and Appeal Board (PTAB)

The inventor and patent professional creates a response to the objections that tries to prove that his invention is indeed patentable and satisfies all patentability criteria's.

Or optionally accepts the objections and amends the patent application as pointed out in examination report.

If USPTO is satisfied with the response to the objections or the amended patent application. Up on finding the patent application in order of grant, The patent is granted to you (inventor) / applicant as early as possible !!!

Involvement:

You (inventor) 30% involvement help patent agent in technical matters of invention (If required) with drafting response for objections.

Patent practitioner 40% involvement to draft the response to objections raised with the help of inventor. Or amend the patent application accordingly. Request for hearing if desired.

USPTO 30% involvement. receive response of objections and decide whether a hearing is needed and whether to grant patent or not

Professional Fees:

The patent agent /attorney may charge a professional fees to respond to objections based on complexity of the objections and number of objections received.

The patent attorney charges anything from $500 to $1500 for response to office action depending up on complexity, subject matter and number of objections.

Step 8: Grant of patent / Notice of Allowance

If the examiner determines that your application is in satisfactory condition and meets the requirements, you will receive a Notice of Allowance.

The notice of allowance will list the issue fee and may also include the publication fee that must be paid prior to the Patent being issued. The patent grant is mailed on the **issue date** of the patent.

The patent is issued in the name of the United States under the seal of the United States Patent and Trademark Office, and is either signed by the Director of the USPTO or is electronically written thereon and attested by an Office official. The patent contains a grant to the patentee, and a printed copy of the specification and drawing is annexed to the patent and forms a part of it.

Description	Fee	Small Entity Fee	Micro Entity Fee
Utility issue fee	1,000.00	500.00	250.00

Involvement:

You (inventor) has 10% involvement patent is granted to you. By paying issue fee you get right to exclude others from using, selling offering for sale, importing your patented invention

Patent practitioner 10% Inform inventor about procedures, renewals and communication to USPTO after grant of patent

USPTO 80% involvement. Grant the patent for invention or reject the patent based on response to objections raised. Giving Notice of Allowance

Patent Maintenance Fees

Description	Fee	Small Entity Fee	Micro Entity Fee
For maintaining an original or any reissue patent, due at 3.5 years	1,600.00	800.00	400.00
For maintaining an original or any reissue patent, due at 7.5 years	3,600.00	1,800.00	900.00
For maintaining an original or any reissue patent, due at 11.5 years	7,400.00	3,700.00	1,850.00

http://patentattorneyworldwide.com/us/

Simplified flow chart from idea to granted patent

Note: for the simplicity of understanding this flow chart does not have provisional patent, international patent, pre grant and post grant oppositions, hearing etc.. mentioned in this flow chart. This is just for simplicity of understanding the overall flow and process.

Complete flow chart from Idea to granted patent

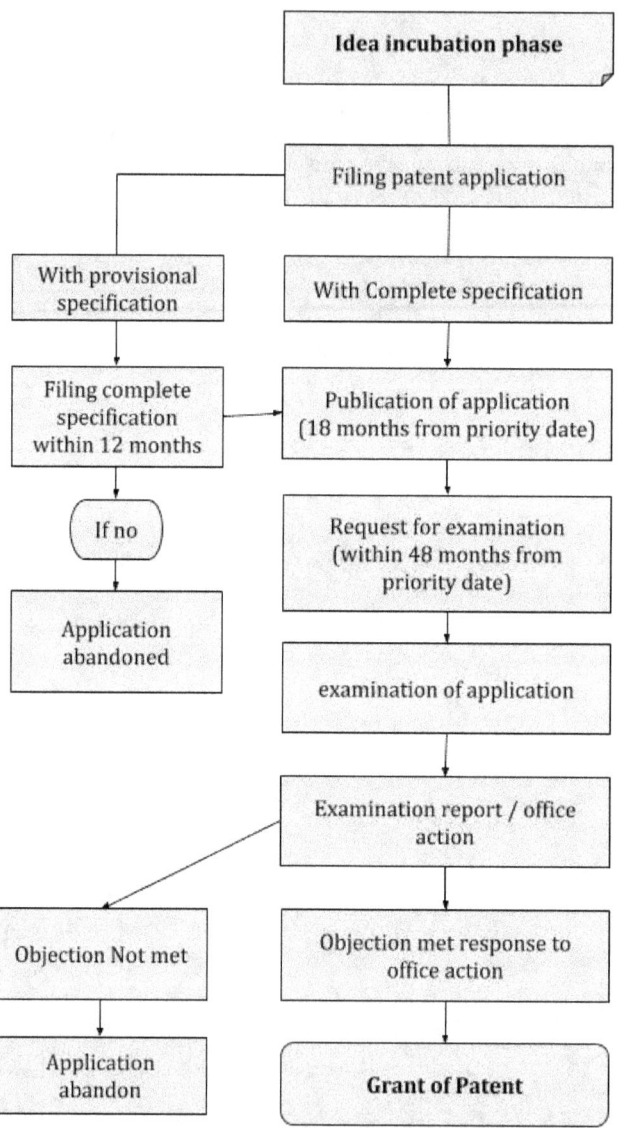

2. Idea incubation phase

Idea Incubation Phase

- How to identify innovative ideas with potential to win patent
- How to do a preliminary search for your innovative idea
- How to review the results you got from this preliminary search
- when to get encouraged and when to get discouraged for going ahead for patent filing based on results
- Creating Final Draft of working invention disclosure
- Mistakes to avoid in Idea incubation phase
- Action items, checklist, worksheet for Idea incubation phase that will help you to create your complete invention disclosure.

"Everything begins with an idea."
– Earl Nightengale

This is probably the most important chapter of the book for you (the inventor) because if you remember when we were going through the steps and procedure for patent at idea incubation phase in your involvement as an inventor is 100% compared to Patent practitioner (not involved yet) and USPTO (not involved yet).

We are looking for a very specific outcome from this section:

The steps here are designed to take your innovative ideas from inception level, that is initial vague ideas about some solution to a problem to a comprehensive invention disclosure (that is ready to discuss with patent agent or attorney) which is the most important starting point the decides the future and fate of your innovative idea.

This is guideline helps you in moving from point A to point B

when you just got an innovative idea that you wish to get patent for	you are ready with comprehensive invention disclosure of your idea

A   **B**

Point A is when you get an innovative idea, and you are thinking to yourself that probably this idea if worked on further could win patent.

Point B is where, you are ready with comprehensive invention disclosure with along with the important information you came across while doing preliminary research about novelty and having closest possible prior arts already identified and included with comprehensive understanding about possible ***novel and non-obvious aspect*** of invention. Hence creating a very informed starting point and invention disclosure that your patent agent / attorney can start working on it right away.

Let's get started,

Get clarity on Idea

We might get more clarity about the innovative ideas when we start writing down things on paper or start typing in a word processor document:

Start taking notes of details about the innovative idea, and get complete idea on a paper or a soft copy document, this is rough draft of your idea and by no means it need to be perfect or complete, just get started with this.

Action Items: Capture all details of idea

- What is my innovative idea is about?
- What problem it solve?
- How does it solve the problem?
- What are some advantages of my innovative idea?
- Technical details about idea and how it function
- Important elements of it
- Block diagram or flow chart or any other relevant diagrams to explain the idea in better way.

Our outcome here is to get down all of our thoughts you need not be perfect or complete initially as there may be plenty of **fill in the blank** elements that you still don't have clarity upon that's pretty natural and we will be filling those elements as and when we proceed.

"this is known as a **brain dump** !!!"

brain-dump is a complete transfer of accessible knowledge about a particular subject from your brain to some other storage medium, such as paper or your computer's hard drive

In the next phase, try to come up with as many diagrams or flowcharts or whatever the convenient way of illustrating and explaining your innovative idea. Again these would be only **rough sketches,** don't worry about the perfection here just get everything in front of you.

Preliminary search

Now, with the idea complete captured, or in some cases the outcome of research and development is completely capture as per actions items above, we are going to perform a small research, we call it as **preliminary search.**

There are two aspects of doing this research:

1. first aspect is try to find if somebody has already developed such an idea; in other words find if it it known to public
2. second aspect is to get a brief idea and understanding about the level of awareness of the market (existing knowledge or state of the art) about your innovative idea.

Here we are trying to understand the **state of the art** or existing knowledge about related to our invention:

so, it is just a preliminary search performed by you (inventor) the objective is just to get the feel of the technology and state of the art (existing knowledge) about your invention, and if possible try to figure out the novel and non obvious aspect of our innovative idea (invention) which is found out by comparing the closest possible prior art (existing knowledge) with our invention and identifying which elements / aspects of our innovative idea are novel and non obvious compared to state of the art.

Now, this is by no means going to replace the comprehensive patentability search performed by a patent agent or attorney.

You may spend around 1 to 3 days to perform preliminary search.

Checklist for doing preliminary search

- How many results we are getting that are really close to our innovative idea or talking something similar to our idea?
- How many products or services are there already in the market that are similar to our invention
- What is the extent of knowledge is already known to public in field of our invention, is there any uniqueness in our innovative idea?
- How our invention is different or better than the prior art... or other products known to public
- Do our idea have novelty? or some part of our invention that is not known to public?

Another important thing is to create and maintain list of keywords that we use to define our innovative idea. You will start with very few keywords, like your version of preferred terms you use for elements,

For example: you would be calling a computer processor as CPU (central procession unit) for our invention, however others may call it a image processor or information processing unit or signal processing system etc...depending on preference of words and language they use, and these all words might be used by different people at different places like articles, blogs, videos, patents, IEEE papers, books to necessarily explain exactly same thing !!!

so to be as comprehensive as possible with our preliminary research we need to build a list of keywords that we used to describe main elements of our innovative idea and its synonyms and other variations that you came across while doing research and reviewing results.

Let's say one of the element is a CCTV camera in our invention, then by finding synonyms for this elements and while doing research we came across different version of names for essentially same or similar device...

see the worksheet below, so updating the list of keywords and synonyms would be **ongoing process** and the list of keywords would keep getting mature and comprehensive as we progress.

List of keywords and synonyms found		
Element 1	**Element 2**	**Element 3**
CCTV system		
Surveillance system		
Camera unit		
Image capturing system		
Video capturing unit		
Live video recording		
Video recorder		
Video sensor		
Image sensor		
Etc…		

Now, preliminary search becomes more and more accurate and shows more relevant results When we start using different combination of keywords from our list. If you able to search with fairly **accurate keyword combinations** related to your idea then chances are you will come across a lot of articles, blogs and sometimes there may be companies and products **very similar to your invention** will show up in the search results.

How to search

- when you have complete information about your invention in front of you; You can start performing search for finding closest possible prior arts
- start with basic keywords and then start adding different variations of keywords using the list of synonyms and different nomenclature that we have enlisted in previous section
- you can start with simple Google search, and slowly build the research on patent specific websites like Google patents, USPTO, European patent search, Indian patent search etc...
- The use of patent classification in searching U.S. patents and published applications usually results in a more comprehensive search than one done by word and phrases (keyword searching).
- Verify the relevancy of CPC classification you found by reviewing the CPC Classification Definition linked to it
- Combine classification search with keyword search to get more specific results
- so probability is you will come across some important prior arts for your innovative idea which are most readily searchable, and easily available on internet

Now, It is important **Not to get discouraged** here seeing a lot of stuff online that is similar to your innovative idea. Keep a good record of the results you feel are very closely related to our invention and create a folder to save these results. We call them closest possible prior arts. Find as many as possible and keep its record, we are going to review them at later stage and these are going to prove important in patent drafting / writing phase as well.

How to review results of preliminary search

Now before we proceed, let me clear it again; we are not replacing a patentability search which is done by patent agent or attorney here. Our only objective is to find the newness of the innovative idea.

If you remember the definition of a patentable invention, As per §35 U.S.C. 101, patentable subject matter is defined as:

"Whoever invents or discovers any new and useful process, machine, manufacture, or composition of matter, or any new and useful improvement thereof may obtain a patent therefor, subject to the conditions and requirements of this title."

And the patentability criteria's
1. novelty
2. non obvious and
3. utility

While reviewing results we are comparing our invention and elements of our invention with the results found (that is prior arts, existing knowledge) and ideally **some aspects** of our invention should be new / novel which is not mentioned in prior art. It is important to know that

"patents are not only given for ground breaking inventions, where as in reality

*patents are granted for **incremental inventions** too. That is incremental improvements in existing systems."*

What we can understand from this (and what is really encouraging) is even if our innovative idea has some aspect that may be very small (yet significant to qualify for patentable invention) you we may win patent for that invention.

In other words, we might have 95% of elements of our invention which are known to public and in existing knowledge. But even if we have 5% of our invention that is some small part of our invention which is novel, which is non-obvious to a person skilled in the art and which has utility then our invention would be patentable !!!

And this is a **great news**... isn't it !!!

What we can learn from this is not to get discouraged seeing thousands of or even lacks of results in your search talking something similar to our invention, our invention still might have something in our invention which could win patent.

When we are reviewing results and closest possible prior arts, look for following things and take a note of it:

find the ways in which your invention is different or rather better in getting intended results or solving existing problem. maybe you have some of points in your inventions as below:
- some aspect of it may be technically advanced or economically significant or both
- Your way to solve the problem is more energy efficient
- your compound, medicine may be having more efficacy
- your software or application is doing some advance things to solve a problem than existing solutions

http://patentattorneyworldwide.com/us/

> **When we are reviewing results**
>
> - Find out how our invention is different or improved in one or the other aspects when we compare it with the prior art
> - Take specific notes of things where our innovative idea solve some problem in existing prior art or the state of the art
> - Particularly look for elements of our invention which are different and which are improved compared to the prior arts found
>
> Take a good note of differences in front of each result after the review so that you can discuss it with patent agent / attorney at appropriate stage.

The improvement may seemingly small but it still can win patent if it is novel, non obvious and is having utility.

It is important to understand **not to get discouraged** while seeing hundreds and thousands of similar patents or articles or blog post talking similar thing like your innovative idea because, there is every chance that you are innovative idea might have at least incremental invention that we could discover at detailed discussion and review with a patent agent /attorney. And a good patent application writing specifically pointing out **novel and non-obvious aspects** of the invention while writing claims would eventually will be rewarded with patent.

Now, you are not expected to do patentability analysis of invention on your own in fact this is done by experienced patent agents and attorneys after performing extensive research for 5 to 7 days, we are not expecting such judgment from you (the inventor).

Instead, we want to address an important problem here that inventor gets discouraged by seeing a lot of results, products, patent and articles in his area and abandons the follow-up or research and development effort although his innovative idea (invention) might be patentable !!!

So, **do not get discouraged** and take next step.

Having said that, there is other side to it as well. When you see that there are many results in the search that talk exactly same like your invention and in fact there are products and services about it being used by public and there is nothing new or improved in your invention when compared to existing knowledge, that is 100% knock out by a single or many prior arts / existing knowledge... then probably yes !!! you may get discouraged and stop following up with that innovative idea. I would still say get opinion from Patent practitioner before you conclude on this too.

At the end of this preliminary search what we have is :

- ✓ a detailed description of invention where every aspect of it is completely captured
- ✓ Diagrams, flowcharts and illustrations if applicable
- ✓ comprehensive list of keywords, synonyms and search terms
- ✓ all results of preliminary search reviewed
- ✓ list of closest possible prior arts
- ✓ differences and problems with prior arts that our invention is solving
- ✓ some aspect of our invention that are novel and non-obvious

having all this information in front of us, now we are in position to create most **comprehensive invention disclosure** also called working disclosure of the invention.

Below are list of questions to which we need to find answers to be able to create a complete invention disclosure

http://patentattorneyworldwide.com/us/

Invention disclosure

Your invention disclosure needs to answer these questions (if not all of them, as many as possible):

- ❏ How you have come up with this innovative idea?
- ❏ What is your invention about?
- ❏ What problem your invention is solving?
- ❏ What are the advantages of your invention?
- ❏ What are important elements or components of your invention?
- ❏ Draw a block diagram or device or flowchart or sketch that explains your invention in better way
- ❏ What products or services that are already in the market which are similar to your invention
- ❏ How your invention is different or improved or efficient than already existing knowledge
- ❏ What components are unique and non-obvious to a person skilled in the art
- ❏ What is the inventive step in your invention that is either technical advanced or economic significance or both
- ❏ Who are the main competitors working in the same field of my innovative idea and what are their products or services
- ❏ Does any publication, articles, news, blog, PDF, book, video or patents completely disclose your invention
- ❏ What part of your invention is crucially important for commercialization
- ❏ How your invention is better than the prior arts and existing knowledge
- ❏ what are the limitations of existing patents or prior art and how your invention is providing solution to those problems
- ❏ can you explain my invention in to granular details such that the disclosure becomes enabling, that is a person skilled in the art should be able to practice their invention without doing additional research just by reading my disclosure of invention.
- ❏ include outcome of experiments or results in table formats, graphs or any charts related to your innovative idea (if applicable)

- ❏ can you mention important elements to be included in claims

although these questions are too much and you probably don't need to answer all of them however you could easily come up with answers to all of them in much better way now... because you have done preliminary search

The collection of information which answers questions above creates a **comprehensive invention disclosure**.

You will have a very important information collected in the folder which would include:

1. Final version of invention disclosure
2. downloaded and reviewed prior art documents
3. your review notes about prior arts mentioning how our invention is different or improved
4. Informed and detailed answers to invention disclosure form
5. your personal notes and opinion about what you think is really novel as per your research and where are **commercial important aspects** of this invention
6. And if possible guideline on **where to focus** when writing and drafting the patent application

Now, when you talk to your patent agent or attorney you know inside out what exactly that you are looking to protect and most important of all you will start with **meaningful discussions** with your patent attorney from the first call itself, simply because the kind of clarity that you have about your invention and the current state of the art related to the field of invention.

How this step will save time and costs

Now having done such an important work on your innovative idea before even contacting to patent agent or attorney (that is following all steps in Idea incubation phase), this will save a lot of efforts, time and ultimately costs when you are moving ahead with patent filing for invention.

Particularly this helps in:

- eliminating a lot of rework / additional research
- to and fro communications and
- delays in communication from your end because you are not prepared with required information

This will drastically reduced it to and fro communications which will really help in reducing the **time and costs to file the patent application** as there would be no rework and crystal clear expectations are set from the word go.

Your patent attorney would appreciate this

And most important of all is your patent agent / attorney going to **love working with you** because you probably are:

- one of the informed client he has came across, and
- he need not educate you while working with you,
- most of patent agents/attorneys would be delighted by the efforts you took to understand the novel and non-obvious part of your invention and coming up with really good invention disclosure
- and may provide you with discounts in the professional fees up to certain extent.

Of course patent agent /attorneys will do their patentability search, they will come up with their own patentability search report and then share it with you and you would be reviewing it with them.

but what you have done for now (in this idea incubation phase) really going to help you in a great deal in getting very close to our **main outcome**, that is "getting the maximum protection for your invention in shortest possible time and at lowest possible cost."

Mistakes to avoid in idea incubation phase

mistake 1: Wasting your valuable time, efforts and money on Innovative ideas that are already known to public.

Taking innovative idea to patent attorney **too early** and directly without doing much of background check. in this case the problem would be wasting time efforts and money on innovative ideas which you yourself would have known prior to giving to patent attorney that the idea is not yet completely developed, or is not at all patentable because this innovative idea is known to public already and was easily discoverable upon doing little bit of research by inventor himself.

Mistake 2: Waiting too long to perfect innovative idea

Second mistake would be analysis paralysis that is waiting for too long to take your innovative ideas to patent agent or attorney. this is the mistake which is initiated by the belief that your inventions should have something groundbreaking new thing to be able to win patent.

Too early and too late both are dangerous when it comes to filing patent application for the invention.

If you are too early, you may be in a ideation stage and research and development still going on, so complete description of invention to get patent might not yet be available with you. hence you might not be protecting the invention with appropriately scope.

And if you are too late, chances are you would lose the priority or even invention since competitors may come up with same patent application before you file one.

3. working with a patent agent or attorney

Save time, costs while working with a patent agent or attorney:

- Do I really need patent agent or patent attorney?
- Can I do it myself, without patent practitioner
- Common mistakes to avoid
- How the Idea incubation phase, if done correctly is really helpful here
- Effective first call or email with a patent agent or attorney firm
- how to Proactively speed up the patenting process
- how to be ready with expected information at appropriate stages
- Opinion about patentability
- Making decision to go ahead with patent filing based on results
- Preparing Patent application (Patent drafting)
- Important rules for patent claims, detailed description, drawings, references, title, Abstract etc.
- Covering all possible embodiments
- How to ensure that the patent application is written to provide **broadest possible protection** for your innovative idea

Do I really need patent agent or patent attorney ?

We will address this question upfront,

The reason behind this question is obvious, you are trying to figure out whether it is worth going for such an expense to go with patent agent / attorney to file a patent application. Or can I just take the forms that are provided, fill in the details and submit it to USPTO? This is basic question that every inventor has when he decides to go ahead for filing patent for his invention.

to answer this question in unbiased way let's take one step back and try to understand who exactly patent practitioner (patent agent or attorney) is...

as you already might be knowing patent is a techno-legal document, as an inventor you are the best person to who understands the invention technically but when it comes to legal as it is a **patent law** (the patent act) you probably won't have that kind of experience or that wisdom to write a patent application considering the legal side of patent.

so let's search few patents from your domain area which is the area of your invention, go on Google patents and try to come up with some granted patents from your domain.

for example you may have mechanical device or idea for software application or E-commerce website to patent. Just type in relevant search keywords and review some results.

Look at the **construction of patent,** have a look at how description is written, how the diagrams are marked and labeled, how detailed the description is written. and then most important part of patent , claims. Observe the language of claims. Structure and order of claim, broader scope claims and narrow claims etc...

You will quickly realize that this is way different than the normal thesis or project report or any technical document you have seen. And there is a reason behind it.

Patents are one of the **most complex documents** involve certain degree of difficulty in creating while considering technical side as well as legal side. After all it is a Law, and like any other law, there are sections, act, rules, general guidelines, case laws, historical wisdom (wisdom from cases and their results) are involved.

So there are way too many aspects, rules, sections and general practices followed by experienced patent practitioners while writing patent application for your invention which is almost impossible to match by a first time inventors.

And interesting thing to know is, USPTO knows that inventors might need help in creating patent application so patent agents and patent attorney are authorized by government to practice before USPTO for patent procedures that is patent prosecution and litigations.

So, registered patent agents and attorneys are made available by USPTO itself to help inventors with patent procedure and help in filing patent for the invention. There is patent bar examination for becoming a registered patent agent which is very difficult level exam.

The main advantage is patent agents and attorneys are also science graduates, like electronics, computer, chemical engineers or pharmaceutical or biotech graduates, so they are equally qualified to understand the technical side of invention as well.

An experienced Patent practitioner stand in your (inventors) shoes and understand invention from your point of view. and he leverage his wisdom of writing patent application as he would have seen hundreds of if not thousands of patents in his career.

Can I do it myself without Patent practitioner ?

It is possible. You can file the patent application without help from Patent practitioner, such application in US called "pro se". Pro Se Assistance Program is for inventors who file patent applications without the assistance of a registered patent attorney or agent (also known as "pro se" filing).

However, USPTO always recommends using a registered attorney or agent to assist in preparing and prosecuting a patent application. This is because writing a good patent application involves **so much more** than a first timer can accommodate into his / her writing, even trained Patent practitioner require at least 3 to 5 years of experience to be able to write reasonably good it in the application. Hence it is worth giving a second thought to it, if you have decided to do it yourself.

"A patent application not written properly, could prove a costly mistake in future as it will not protect your invention as you expected it to do and it will probably not worth the time and effort and costs you put to get the invention protected."

There are rules about so many things while writing patent application:
- ✓ Rules about writing title of image
- ✓ rules for writing abstract
- ✓ how claims should be written
- ✓ how detailed description is to be written
- ✓ rules for drawings
- ✓ rules for numbering the drawings
- ✓ rules for pages

it is very likely that the first time inventor or do-it-yourself patent writer would be making some **obvious mistakes** that could prove costly in the longer term. Hence, if your invention is worth patenting it probably is worth having a patent agent or attorney.

Hiring a skilled patent practitioner, even if only to consult, would help in avoiding costly mistakes that could occur (if you take do it yourself approach).

Common mistake if you are do it yourself

Some common mistakes done by inventors while writing and filing patent application on their own are:

- The disclosure of invention is not sufficient enough and not enabling
- Claims are not supported in description of the invention
- Claims are not protecting the actual inventions properly
- The inventive feature is not properly claimed
- The claims written are too limiting and lack the proper legal terms to be able to have border scope
- All possible variations and embodiments are not mentioned
- Best mode of practicing invention is not disclosed

And this list by no means complete, and many other type of mistakes that can raise a lot of **objections (office action) in the proceeding** of getting patent for your invention.

Having said that It has been observed that some inventors have written their patent application with remarkable quality and understanding of legal aspect of writing that it is hard to believe it is not written by an experienced patent attorney but by an inventor. However such cases are **very rare** and most often than not, inventors understand the technology part really well and but lack the understanding of legal aspects when writing patent application especially writing claims for the invention.

Writing patent application is a specialized skill

Writing patent application requires fair understanding and experience in

- Patent law and USPTO rules and regulations
- Case laws affecting the interpretation of patent law
- Technical skills of subject matter of the invention

As an inventor you can be a leading expert in your field of invention that is technical side of it that's your strength but where you may face challenge is legal side of it. Without (patent attorney or patent agent) chances are your patent application would be **just a technical description of the invention** and may fail for its sole purpose of "protecting your invention with broadest possible scope" refer our outcome expected from patent in introduction.

When you (inventor) work with right patent attorney (agent), it becomes a combination of your technical expertise + patent attorneys legal expertise and this can result into a very strong patent that adequately protects every aspect of your invention.

http://patentattorneyworldwide.com/us/

Advantages of going with patent agent or attorney

1. Patent agent and attorney would know how to write patent application and claims to have the **broadest possible protection** for your invention such that your competitors should not be able to copy your invention or just walk around your invention by changing some things and not infringing on your patent.

2. Writing a patent application itself has extensive laws, rules and procedures applicable, and number of things to consider, you would be surprised to know, there are rules related to margins of the page, rules for writing the title, abstract, claims, diagrams, detailed description, enabling etc...

3. The entire process of inception of idea to granted patent and beyond becomes a smooth experience for you when you have experienced patent agent / attorney guiding you at every stage...

what do you mean by objections raised, how to respond to objections etc... all these kind of things are already taken care by patent agent or attorney and not to forget the importance of dates and subsequent steps you should be considering for entire procedure.

so patent attorney takes care of reminding you for every date and appropriate steps to be taken with right information.

So, these 3 things makes this investment in going for patent agent or attorney look pretty small if you are considering in the longer term that is the life of your invention and if at all you win the patent get 20 years from the filing date that you are going to enjoy monopoly on it.

ultimately it depends on level of seriousness that you have with your invention (and of course your budget).

You can definitely leverage tutorials and guidelines or books on writing patent application and do it on your own and file it at USPTO and see what happens with the objections raised after examination of application.

And worst of all

"you may get the patent granted for your invention which you written on your own but when it comes to monetizing or commercializing the patent in the market, you may find out that you **failed to** protect your invention with fullest scope, or the claims of patent have no commercial value in the market."

In other words, even though you have a granted patent for your invention, you do not have the broadest possible protection for your invention as patent application and especially claims are written by inexperienced inventor himself or herself... and **you would not be able to stop others** from competing with your invention without infringing on your patent.

Hence an experienced patent practitioner with years of experience would know what is commercially important aspects of your invention and how to write patent application that would

1. Provide broadest possible scope for our invention
2. Competitors should not be able to copy or compete with our invention without our consent
3. Competitors should not be able to work around our patented invention and build similar solution without infringing on our patent (this is most important expectation)
    a. we should be able to monetize the patented invention by
    b. by producing patented invention without worrying about competition
    c. by licensing it to other company to get royalty payments

4. by completely selling the patent rights to other business and get significant monetary benefits for your efforts

if you are serious with your invention and don't want to lose its entire Novelty or **don't want to lose upon the opportunity** to take it to the next level then you should consider hiring a patent agent or attorney. It is well worth the investment.

On the other hand; you can try writing and filing patent application on your own but as explained above it is really difficult if not impossible to match the level of well drafted patent application by an expert Patent practitioner, and more often than not you will end up losing on the opportunity to protect your invention adequately and making significant money with it.

that's why patent agents and patent attorneys are there to help and they improve your chances to getting patent granted for your invention.

The responsibilities of patent agent / attorney

- Representing clients in all matters and procedures relating to patent
- Preparing application for patent
- Providing advice during patent application process
- Helps in drafting strong claims for your invention to be able to protect it in fullest possible extent
- prosecuting patent applications

By executing power of attorney, you (inventor) can appoint a patent attorney or agent to represent you for patent proceedings at USPTO.

First meeting with patent attorney

It always start with a Non disclosure agreement (NDA).

A non disclosure agreement is an agreement that patent agent / attorney or Intellectual Property firm is doing with you, for keeping the confidentiality of your invention.

In other words the Patent practitioner doing this non disclosure agreement with you (inventor) and agreeing on keeping your invention confidential / secret and do not misuse it.

There are **no cost** or charges for doing this agreement, however it is a strong document which you can take it to court your invention is misused by the Patent practitioner (but this almost never happens)

The first meeting with patent agent or attorney could be in person or communication on call or via emails. The first thing always remains same, signing Non disclosure agreement with inventor to keep the invention confidential.

effective first meeting with Patent practitioner

To have an effective first meeting with Patent practitioner you should be ready with:

- a detailed description of invention where every aspect of it is completely captured
- Diagrams, flowcharts and illustrations if applicable
- comprehensive list of keywords, synonyms and search terms
- list of closest possible prior arts
- differences and problems with prior arts that our invention is solving
- other products or services in market that are similar to our invention
- our competitor working in same field
- what feature is novel and non obvious
- commercially important feature to protect
- sample claims from your point of view

along with all the relevant answers to question from invention disclosure form

This is where **our idea incubation phase** helps us to be well prepared and it becomes an easy job for us now… all we need to do is share the outcome documents that we have prepared from the idea incubation phase along with the closest possible prior arts that we have identified.

Ideally Patent agent or attorney would like to go through all this information **before** having meeting with you such that the meeting becomes fruitful and result oriented.

It is important for you to understand that all the information that is relevant to the innovative ideas should be disclosed to the patent attorney sometimes seemingly un-important or trivial information **could prove important** in the context of the invention.

sometimes patent attorney might ask you to illustrate **entire timeline starting with Idea** and the action steps that you took to develop the innovative idea into current state, this time line discussion also includes technical details of the invention, its features and advantages, the problem invention solve, and how it is different or better than prior arts already known to public.

Another important aspect of this first meeting with patent attorney is to get **working invention disclosure** having sufficient information about the innovative idea such that it becomes **enabling**, and person skilled in the art would be able to practice their invention based on the disclosure. And with the detailed invention disclosure Patent practitioner could perform the comprehensive Novelty / Patentability search.

It is important to discuss all the **synonyms** and different set of **keywords used to identify the same element** of the invention, here again or preparation that we did in Idea incubation phase comes to rescue and we are already ready with all the synonyms and parallel words used for different elements of our invention.

Many times it is important for patent attorney to understand whether the elements of the invention could be replaced with something similar and still the performs its intended purpose? List down all such elements that could be replaced so as to form the highest possible protection while writing claims and detailed description of the invention.

Identify the novel feature or novel part of the invention along with identifying commercially important element of the invention.

Drafting the first claim in the meeting itself

If we have performed all the steps correctly tin now, and have communicated all results to patent agent or attorney **before the meeting** for review (of course after signing NDA online or via email) then this step is possible.

It would be really helpful if a patent attorney could draft the first claim (first independent claim) for your invention during the first meeting itself, as most of the description in the patent application follows the claims, it would be a great achievement if you and patent agent or attorney could write the first set of claims in the first meeting itself. Of course the claim would be revised and updated but if we could get finalized set of at least first independent claim in first meeting itself when you and patent attorney are together then this would be a great head start for moving towards filing patent application for your invention.

This step will **greatly enhance the speed** of completing patent application as having finalized set of claims ready will make the job of writing the patent application easier and less time consuming.

Patentability search or Novelty search

This would be a comprehensive search performed by patent practitioners to find out patentability of your innovative idea. Similar to the brief preliminary search that we have performed in the idea incubation phase, this search also have the objective to find out the closest possible prior art related to our invention.

but unlike our brief search the patent practitioner goes into most comprehensive and detailed search as possible. The patentability search involves

The patentability search involves

- advance keyword search tactics
- classification search
- search by company name or assignee
- combination of different strategies in a single search query
- searching forward and backward referenced of a good prior art
- search in different patent databases
- Patent applications that are published
- Patents that are granted
- non-patent literature like articles blogs websites
- IEEE papers and non patent literature search
- products and services available in market
- and other relevant the platforms in the domain of your invention

and it takes about 4-6 days for a Patent practitioner to do a comprehensive patentability search and create a **Patentability search report.**

In the report the results of this patentability search are closely analyzed and map against the elements of our invention. It is important responsibility of inventor to help patent attorney to identify how our invention is different and or improved from the results that are cited in the patentability search report.

Ideal case would be some aspect of our invention is are **solving a long standing problem** that the prior art patents failed to solve. This would prove a strong evidence to **prove non obviousness** of our invention.

Opinion on patentability

Based on the result on patentability search patent attorney give an opinion about the patentability of your innovative idea:

- **Negative opinion:** If there are results in patentability search report which are similar to your invention and there is no novelty in your innovative idea compared to existing knowledge. That is the innovative idea is already known to public and there is no novelty; then a patent agent or attorney might advise you not to go for patent. This will save you a lot of time and costs that you otherwise would be incurring on filing patent application for an idea which would not result in granted patent.

- **Neutral opinion:** in this case the patent agent / attorney is of opinion that your invention stands a fair chance of winning patent for some aspects of your invention which are found to be novel and having inventive step based on results in patentability search. You may receive some objections from USPTO yet by responding to it you may get patent for your invention.

- **Positive opinion:** this is when your invention has some features that are novel and non obvious when compared with existing knowledge and prior arts found in the patentability report. This is a positive sign and patent agent or attorney might advise you to go ahead for patent filing.

Advantages of patentability search

- Patentability search help us in identifying the closest possible prior arts which are likely to be found by examiner at the examination stage of the patent application. Hence considering these prior art before writing patent application **increase chances of getting patent granted**.

- The identified prior arts are mentioned in the references and our invention is established as solution to long standing problem which is not yet solved. such an approach creates good chances of proving inventive feature that is the solution our invention has provided was not obvious to a person skilled in the art as the problem is existed for so long. Hence it is **useful in proving novelty and inventive step** which improves chances of getting patent granted for our invention.

- And ultimately patentability search also **saves lot of unnecessary costs**, efforts and procedures in filing the patent application for invention which doesn't stand a chance of surviving patentability criteria and would be rejected anyway.

Preparing Patent application (patent drafting)

Let's review our expectation from a patent application one more time.

The outcome expected from Patent protection

- ✓ Provide broadest possible protection to our innovative ideas
- ✓ Competitors should not be able to copy or compete with our invention without our consent
- ✓ Competitors should not be able to work around our patented invention and build similar solution without infringing on our patent (this is most important point)
- ✓ we should be able to monetize the patented invention by
    - o by producing patented invention without competition
    - o by licensing it to other company to get royalty payments
    - o by completely selling the patent rights to other business
and get significant monetary benefits for your efforts

writing a patent application around the novel feature of the invention needs very balanced and scientific approach which has to take in account the technical as well as legal side.

Going too broad or too narrow protection while writing claims would be a mistake.

"Claims should not be too broad because those would be anticipated by existing prior arts, and the claims should not be too narrow because competitors would be easily able to work around our invention"

Now as an inventor or applicant of patent **you are not supposed to know all these rule and skills for patent drafting**, As teaching details about drafting a patent application or claim drafting is outside the scope of this book. And honestly it would be impossible to acquire those skills by mere reading a book (as discussed in detailed manner in previous section) so we would be brief about this.

The purpose of this section is to **make you (inventor) aware** about:
- what happens at every stage, behind the scene actions happing with your invention disclosure,
- what to expect at each stage,
- being prepared with required information,
- things to ensure in a quality draft and
- minimize mistakes along the way.

We will start form where we left from the last section 'the patentability opinion'. After receiving neutral or positive patentability opinion form patent agent / attorney, you take a decision whether to proceed with the patent drafting and patent filing process. depending up on:

- the type of patent application (provisional or complete)
- only US application or international patent application (PCT or convention)
- complexity of subject matter
- preparedness of inventor with required information (invention disclosure) and
- available time / bandwidth of patent practitioner to work on your project (along with other projects)

it takes about 5 to 12 days for a patent agent or patent attorney to come up with a draft of patent application, which you review along with him.

http://patentattorneyworldwide.com/us/

Patent drafting how Patent practitioner does it

You may be surprised to know, the patent drafting does not begin with title of the invention or the abstract; In fact most Patent practitioner first draft claims !!!

Claims are most important part of patent application.

- ❏ Claims decide the boundaries of the protection that you would be getting for your invention
- ❏ Claims are used to enforce your patent
- ❏ Claims decide whether the competitor is infringing on your patent
- ❏ Claim are closely examined in the patent examination phase at USPTO
- ❏ Claims are most difficult part of patent application to write

Of course, there are other dependencies and rules for other parts of patent applications when deciding scope but it is the claim which stands most important thing that decides the future of your patent.

Important things about claims:

The purpose of claim is to define the invention protected by the patent.

The reason patent agent or attorney starts with writing claims first, because once we have complete set of claims providing appropriate protection to the invention and which are approved by you (inventor), then writing remaining parts of the patent application like: detailed description, abstract and summary becomes easier as these parts generally follow the boundaries set by claims.

How to review claims

To be honest, a patent agent or attorney is the most appropriate person to write and review claims with you, however there are some important things to consider :

- Since, claims define the scope of legal protection, it is suggested that they should be drafted carefully to cover all the aspects of the protection being sought at the same time adequately distinguishing the prior art from the claimed invention.
- Unity of invention and clarity of claims
    - a) Claim(s) of a Complete Specification shall relate to a single invention, or to a group of inventions linked so as to form a single inventive concept.
    - b) Claims shall be clear and succinct and fairly based on the matter disclosed in the specification.
- Rules for writing preamble such that it should not be limiting the scope of invention
- Rules about using appropriate transition like "comprising" "consisting of"
- What is not claimed in the claims stands disclaimed, and is open to public use, even if the matter is disclosed in the description.
- Each claim is evaluated on its own merit and, therefore, if one of the claims is objected, it does not mean that the rest of the claims are invalid.
- it is therefore important to make claims on all aspects of the invention to ensure that the applicant gets the widest possible protection.

And there are many rules and standard practices that a professional would be incorporating while writing claims for your patent application. In short,

"Claims should be written in such a way that they would not be invalidated in the litigation phase and they would not allow competitors to practice the invention without infringing on patented invention"

http://patentattorneyworldwide.com/us/

Important things about drawings:

It is required to include the drawings which helps in explaining the invention wherever it is appropriate to do so, if not done the patent application would be rejected or requires submission of relevant drawings describe the invention.

- the drawing plays much more important role than just illustrating the invention to be patented.
- the drawings are also used to define the scope of the disclosure of the invention and claims of the invention.
- If in case your invention disclosure has not explicitly included some features of the invention but they are present in the drawings of your invention, then the drawings can be used as a basis to support the claim that talks about that particular feature. In other words claims can find support in drawings even though it is not explicitly mentioned in the detailed description of the invention

hence it is important to consider drawing as a significant part of patent application and it is required to handle it with care while writing the patent application.

Even though you do not want to go for professional drawings (which is recommended to do) you can submit hand drawn sketches along with the patent application as long as those sketches are readable, can be comprehended and related to the invention disclosure. such hand-drawn sketches are called **informal drawings**. but it is recommended to go for formal drawings as long as possible.

in general drawing include:

- Flowcharts
- Graphs
- Tables
- perspective view of device
- front view
- top view
- side view of Elements

- the sectional views of elements
- illustrations of invention in use

And Just like claims and drawings there are many rules and standards for writing other elements of patent specification like:

- Title of the invention
- Abstract
- Background of the invention
- references
- Detailed description
- Field of invention
- Include references to cite
- disclosing best mode
- covering all possible embodiments

and many more...

however discussing all the rules and regulation is outside the scope of this book and its outcome. Still if you are interested in reading them, below are the documents on USPTO website you can download and read...

Appendix L Patent Laws
United States Code Title 35 - Patents

Appendix R Consolidated Patent Rules

Manual of Patent Examining Procedure

https://www.uspto.gov/patent website under resources section

How patent attorney works on your invention

when you think about **near perfect patent application** that properly protect your invention, there are few things a patent application should do:

- The claims for invention written in appropriate manner such that claims are broad enough to stop competitors from working around the invention and at the same time claims are narrow enough not to be anticipated by existing prior art
- Describing the invention in enough detailed manner such that the person skilled in the art should be able to understand and practice the invention, that is it should be enabling description of the invention.
- All possible variation and embodiments of the invention are covered.
- Claiming the invention in such a way that it will survive not only prosecution (that is till the grant) but also it will survive the litigation phase (after the grant). And licensing phase (that is making money with patented invention)
- Describing the best mode of practicing the invention
- and in case you (inventor) decides to go for foreign filing a patent application should be able to facilitate foreign filing/ international filing.
- and of course the patent application should be following all the rules and laws about how patent application should be written as required by patent law.

based on all of these input the patent attorney creates the final draft of the patent application along with the drawings to be reviewed by inventor. And upon receiving the final draft of the patent application you (inventor) should review it line by line keeping in mind the scope of your invention that you want to be protected.

all the corrections that is adding information removing information or editing existing information is to be done with track changes enabled document editor, search that your corrections would be appropriately grasped by patent agent or attorney. and after considering suggestions and changes the patent application is ready to be filed in USPTO.

Proactively speeding up the process

In general it takes from 2 to 5 years to have a patent granted. There are many strategies and ways to speed up this process and get patent granted in less time. Some strategies for things to do before filing patent application and some are applicable after filing patent application

1. **Strategies to speed up before filing patent application:**

   - being ready with appropriate information about the invention really reduces time from ideation stage of invention to patent filed stage of invention, Idea incubation phase and preliminary search help in great deal to speed things up and shorten the time and frequency of communication with Patent practitioner
   - drafting first claim in the meeting with patent agent or attorney which helps in creating rest of the patent application in quicker time. Saving a lot of emails and meetings for same outcome.
   - Directly filing complete patent application, without spending time in patentability search or provisional patent application

The main theme remains being prepared with information and taking proactive steps to minimize the delay at all intermediate steps.

To accelerate the patent examination process, USPTO offers the provision of speeding up the patent examination process as follows :

1. Prioritized examination
2. Accelerated examination
3. First action interview pilot program
4. Patent prosecution highway
5. Petition to make special

https://www.uspto.gov/patent

4. Filing Patent application

Filing Patent application:

- Different options, paths and strategies for Filing patent application
- Provisional patent application
- When to go for provisional patent application
- advantages
- mistakes to avoid
- Non provisional (Complete) patent application
- International patent application
- different options and routes available
- strategies to go about international patent filing
- Patent Cooperation Treaty (PCT) application
- Advantages of PCT over convention application
- Fees for PCT application

Patent filing

Once you and your patent attorney approves the final version of patent application it is filed at USPTO as soon as possible.

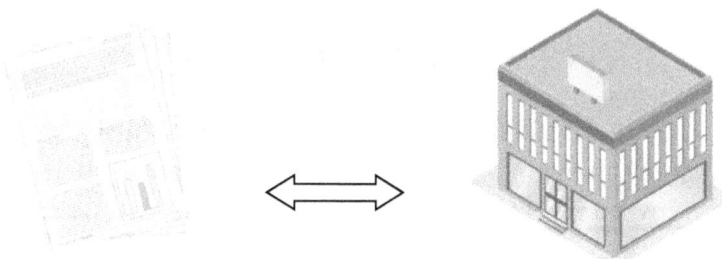

There are many options and routes for filing patent application based on following things:

- the stage of your invention
- the country of your interest for getting patent protection
- number of countries of your interest forgetting pattern protection outside US
- your budget for filing patent application/

Types of patent applications

1. Provisional patent application

A provisional application is filed when you are not quite ready with your invention and you want to borrow the time to work further on research and development of your invention and at the same time you don't want to lose on priority date. A provisional specification may or may not have claims.

Filing provisional application gives you 12 months of time within which you need to file non-provisional (complete) patent application. If you fail to file complete patent application within 12 months from the filing of provisional patent application your application will be abandoned.

2. Non- provisional (Complete) patent application

The complete application / specification describes the invention fully and completely along with the best mode and complete set of claims the complete specification includes following elements explained in details in section below:

3. Convention Application

When an applicant files the application for a patent, claiming a priority date based on similar application filed in convention countries, it is called a convention application.

You can file the application in the USPTO within twelve months from the date of first filing of a similar application in the convention country.

4. Patent Cooperation Treaty (PCT) – International Application

It is an international agreement for filing patent applications having effect in up to 150 countries.

"PCT is administered by World Intellectual Property Organization WIPO, and it's primary objective is to provide a system where you need to make only one patent application which would be searched by at least one International search authority and examined by at least one selected International preliminary Examination Authority IPEA"

It is important to remember that pct does not provide the grant of patent it only facilitates single application which would be taken from searching to examination stage centrally and which would be applicable for all the signatory countries in pct. Currently number of countries associated in PCT are 150.

The application is to be filed in English language within 12 months from the date of filing in US.

5. PCT-National Phase Application

This is an application filed in USPTO claiming the priority of international filing date is called PCT National Phase application.

First the international application is made as per (PCT) and then the first application, can enter the national phase in US within 30 months from the international filing date or priority date (whichever is earlier).

Provisional patent application

When you are at a stage in your research and development work where, it can be disclosed on paper but it's not a final invention, then you can prepare a description of the invention as provisional specification and submit to USPTO to secure the priority date of the invention.

It gives following benefits:

- ✓ Secures filing date
- ✓ 12 months of time to file complete specification
- ✓ Low upfront cost

When you complete the required documents and your research work then you can file complete specification.

Filing the provisional specification is an **optional step**, if you are at the stage where you have complete information about your invention then you can directly go for complete specification.

A provisional application for patent (provisional application) is a U.S. national application filed in the USPTO under 35 U.S.C. §111(b).

A provisional application do not require:
- a formal patent claim
- an oath or declaration
- Provisional applications need not include prior arts

since provisional applications are not examined.

Important things to remember about provisional patent application:

- A provisional specification is not a rough draft;

- it defines the field of invention and also defines the scope of the invention to certain extent.
- Even if you file complete specification later it does not replace the provisional specification, it still remains in the record.
- The USPTO accords the filing date and patent application number to the provisional specification received.
- If the complete specification is not filed within 12 months from the filing date of provisional specification, the patent application is treated as deemed to have been abandoned.

Provisional application should include:

filing fee

Large entity	Small entity	Micro entity
$280	$140	$70

a cover sheet identifying:

- the application as a provisional application for patent;
- the names of all inventors;
- inventor residences;
- title of the invention;
- name and registration number of attorney or agent and docket number (if applicable);
- correspondence address; and
- any U.S. Government agency that has a property interest in the application.

How filing provisional application could help?

If we see a typical life cycle of a patent owner, the most preferred way you get your ROI with the patents is by licensing it to other business. The Success in licensing your patent to other business lies in commercial potential of your invention and your ability to commercialize it, how you talk to decision makers and project the advantages and potential profits by licensing rights for your patented invention.

So, instead of going for complete patent application, you can choose to go with provisional patent application as a low cost starting option and leverage the 12 months time to test the commercial potential of the invention by talking to companies who could be interested in licensing your patent.

Advantages of Provisional patent application

- **Low upfront cost:** you end up paying much less for filing a provisional application than filing a complete patent application.
- You can write **"Patent Pending"** status: Although provisional patent is not actually a patent and it will not be converted to complete patent application unless you take further steps... You legally can write "Patent Pending" for your invention. (product prototype) up on filing provisional patent you have secured the priority date as its filing date, so you need not worry about confidentiality.
- **Time to let invention Evolve:** Filing a complete patent application at very early stage of the invention could be a mistake and it may not protect your invention adequately, so filing provisional application secures your priority date and gives you enough time to work on your invention to the fullest possible potential.
- **Time to test the commercial potential:** Having secured the priority date by filing a provisional application, you can test few things like:
    o Willingness of other businesses to license your invention then patented
    o Get an understanding about commercial worth of invention

http://patentattorneyworldwide.com/us/

- Time to conduct market research and test commercial potential
- In effect you get full 12 months of time to decide whether to move ahead with complete patent application or not, as during this period you can do extensive market research and find the commercial worth of your invention without worrying about its confidentiality.

- **abandon the provisional patent application:** (saves you money) In case you happened to find out that the invention for which you already have filed provisional patent application is not worth going ahead for full patent protections for some reasons like:
  - The invention is not worth that much commercially
  - No one willing to buy, license it neither you willing to produce the invention, etc.

  You actually **save thousands of rupees**, you otherwise would have spent on directly going for complete patent application, and if at all decided to abandon it in between for some reasons.

- **Becomes granted Patent:** (by following procedure) the provisional patent can become granted patent if the complete patent application is filled within 12 months from filing date of provisional patent and entire patent procedure is followed till grant of patent. (Provided the patent application is not rejected by the controller)

Now, the granted patent will have the benefit of earlier priority date (that is filing date of provisional patent) as **priority date is crucially important** in all stages of patent life cycle, right from examination stage to grant of patent and even in litigations stage and even while monetizing patent.

Mistakes to avoid in Provisional Application

Be careful when writing provisional application for your invention.

- **It is a scope defining document:** A provisional application is not a rough draft of your idea or invention. In fact it defines the scope of your invention. So every part (element) of your invention which is outside the scope of the provisional application and you happened to develop in the 12 months time (that is at the time of filing complete patent application) will fail to have the earlier priority date (filing date of provisional application). Which means the part of invention you developed after filing provisional which is outside the scope which is set by provisional application will not have the advantage of priority date of provisional application.
- Even if you file complete specification later it does not replace the provisional specification, **it still remains in the record**. The USPTO allocates the filing date and patent application number to the provisional application received.
- If the complete specification is not filed within 12 months from the filing date of provisional specification, the patent application is treated as deemed to have been **abandoned**.
- Another mistake would be failing to disclose the scope of invention.
- **The description of invention should not be limiting:** The language used in patent application plays an important role in defining its scope: While writing description for invention, you should avoid using limiting words like "must have" "consists" "essential" Instead try to describe elements of the invention with as broad scope as possible: You can use terms like a "writing device" instead of directly saying "a pen" which would be of limiting scope and can eliminate other writing devices like pencil from the scope.
- publically disclosing parts of invention that are not protected by provisional specification. This would destroy the novelty of the part of invention which is not covered in provisional specification

So, in a way provisional patent application is **a way to save costs** while protecting your innovative idea meanwhile. If you utilize it in certain way, it is indeed a low upfront cost option that give you time to test the true potential of the invention before actually going for full patent procedure. additionally your **priority date is secured** and the **confidentiality** is taken care.

Non provisional patent application

A non-provisional utility patent application to be filed at USPTO must include

- a specification,
- a description,
- at least one claim;
- drawings (if required),
- an oath or declaration; and
- the prescribed filing, search, and examination fees.

An **oath** or declaration is a formal statement that you believe that you are the original inventor of the claimed invention in the application, and the statement that the application was made by you (the inventor).

Fees

Large entity	Small entity	Micro entity
$300	$150	$75

fees for filing, searching, examining, issuing, appealing, and maintaining patent applications and patents are reduced by **50 percent for any small entity** that qualifies for reduced fees under 37 CFR § 1.27(a),

and are reduced by **75 percent for any micro entity** that files a certification that the requirements under 37 CFR § 1.29(a) or (d) are met.

Prefer filing electronically via EFS-Web to save costs (fees). If you file your non-provisional utility application in paper by mail or by hand-delivery; additional non-electronic filing fee of $400 ($200 for small and micro entities) needed to pay on top of the regular filing, search, and examination fees.

If fees for filing, search, or examination is paid on a date later than the patent application filing date would require a late surcharge of $160, $80 for small entity and $40 for micro entity.

Hence, your best and economic option would be file non provisional utility patent application electronically via EFS-Web along with pay filing, search, and examination fees at the time of filing itself.

If a postcard is submitted with a patent application, the detailed listing should include the following items:

- title and number of pages of each USPTO form
- number of pages of specification (excluding claims)
- number of claims and the number of claim pages
- number of figures of drawing and the number of sheets of drawings
- whether an oath or declaration statement is included and the number of pages
- type and number of other documents that are included and the number of pages of each document
- amount of payment and the method of payment (i.e., check, credit card, money order, or USPTO deposit account)

Patent co-operation treaty (PCT)

As explained earlier patents are territorial. that means if you have patent for your invention in United States (US) you cannot stop someone from making using selling offering for sale or importing your patented invention in some other country, that is other than US.

Now you may want to go for as many countries as possible to protect your invention.

If you go by traditional way (that is by paris convention) you need to file patent applications in all countries of your interest within 12 months from the date of filing of patent application in your home country.

The Paris Convention *is an international treaty that allows applicants to file a first application in their home country. And within 12 months period further application called a Paris Convention application could be filed at desired countries.*

Now for example you selected 10 countries to file your patent application, can you imagine the simultaneous workload? doing all the steps in all the countries of your interest like replying to objections, request for examinations, translating your patent application into different languages and ultimately professional charges of patent agents or attorneys involved at different patent offices and all this happening **simultaneously** !!!

this is what would happen if you take the traditional route for international filing of your patent application. to avoid such chaotic condition expenses and additional workload **patent cooperation treaty** created.

The Patent Cooperation Treaty (PCT) is an international treaty with more than 150 Contracting States. The granting of patents remains under the control of the national or regional patent offices in what is called the "national phase".

"PCT is administered by World Intellectual Property Organization WIPO, and it's primary objective is to provide a system where you need to make only one patent application which would be searched by at least one International search

authority and examined by at least one selected International preliminary Examination Authority IPEA"

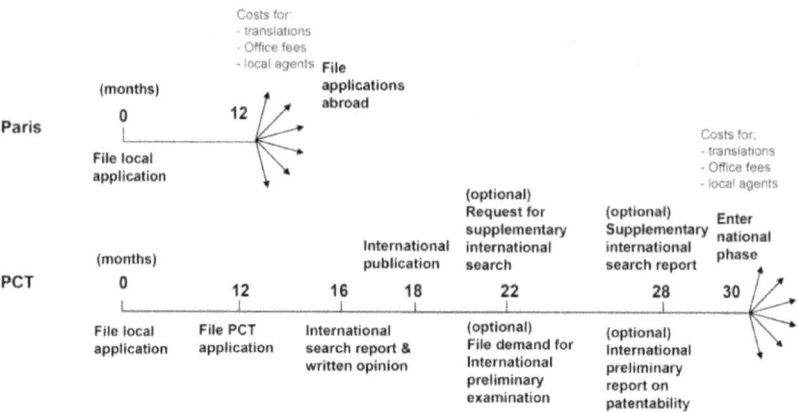

It is important to remember that pct does not provide the grant of patent it only facilitates single application which would be taken from searching to examination stage centrally and which would be applicable for all the signatory countries in pct. Currently number of countries associated in PCT are 150.

The PCT makes it possible to apply for patent protection for your invention simultaneously in a large number of countries by filing a single "international" patent application instead of filing several separate national or regional patent applications (as in case with convention patent application).

when you file International patent application to PCT, unlike the previous (convention application) option, your international patent application is valid for all 150 member countries of PCT (that is up to international phase) and here you have about 30 to 31 months of time to decide whether to enter into the national phase of the country of the interest.

This decision depends on the international search and examination report.

International phase is the phase during which the international patent application is published, search and examined before entry in designated country (that is national phase)

National phase is the phase when International patent application enter in the countries of interest. The international patent application is searched and examined by National patent offices and its granted or rejected

The PCT procedure includes:

- **Filing:** you file an international application with a national or regional patent Office or WIPO, complying with the PCT formality requirements, in one language, and you pay one set of fees.
- **International Search:** an "International Searching Authority" (ISA) (one of the world's major patent Offices) identifies the published patent documents and technical literature ("prior art") which may have an influence on whether your invention is patentable, and establishes a written opinion on your invention's potential patentability.
- **International Publication:** as soon as possible after the expiration of 18 months from the earliest filing date, the content of your international application is disclosed to the world.
- **Supplementary International Search (optional):** a second ISA identifies, at your request, published documents which may not have been found by the first ISA which carried out the main search because of the diversity of prior art in different languages and different technical fields.
- **International Preliminary Examination (optional):** one of the ISAs at your request, carries out an additional patentability analysis, usually on an amended version of your application.
- **National Phase:** after the end of the PCT procedure, usually at 30 months from the earliest filing date of your initial application, from which you claim priority, you start to pursue the grant of your patents directly before the national (or regional) patent Offices of the countries in which you want to obtain them.

Advantages of PCT over convention application

advantages of pct application over convention application:

- The pct provides most effective and most economic way of filing patent application in multiple countries
- It enables the application to file single patent application with single patent office in single language having effect in each country to pct
- The application is searched by international search authority
- It provides formal examination of international application by an international preliminary examination authority
- centralized International Publication of international patent application
- reduced load on patent officers by taking international patent application through searching and examination before entering in to the national phase

Fees for PCT application

PCT Fees - National Stage

Description	Fee	Small Entity Fee	Micro Entity Fee
Basic National Stage Fee	300.00	150.00	75.00
National Stage Search Fee - U.S. was the ISA or IPEA and all claims satisfy PCT Article 33(1)-(4)	0.00	0.00	0.00
National Stage Search Fee - U.S. was the ISA	140.00	70.00	35.00
National Stage Search Fee - search report prepared and provided to USPTO	520.00	260.00	130.00
National Stage Search Fee - all other situations	660.00	330.00	165.00
National Stage Examination Fee - U.S. was the ISA or IPEA and all claims satisfy PCT Article 33(1)-(4)	0.00	0.00	0.00
National Stage Examination Fee - all other situations	760.00	380.00	190.00
Each independent claim in excess of three	460.00	230.00	115.00
Each claim in excess of 20	100.00	50.00	25.00
Multiple dependent claim	820.00	410.00	205.00
Search fee, examination fee or oath or declaration after the date of commencement of the national stage	140.00	70.00	35.00
English translation after thirty months from priority date	140.00	70.00	35.00
National Stage Application Size Fee - for each additional 50 sheets that exceeds 100 sheets	400.00	200.00	100.00

PCT Fees - International Stage

Description	Fee	Small Entity Fee	Micro Entity Fee
Transmittal fee	240.00	120.00	60.00
Non-electronic filing fee (additional fee for applications filed in paper)	400.00	200.00	200.00
Search fee - regardless of whether there is a corresponding application (see 35 U.S.C. 361(d) and PCT Rule 16)	2,080.00	1,040.00	520.00
Supplemental search fee when required, per additional invention	2,080.00	1,040.00	520.00
Transmitting application to Intl. Bureau to act as receiving office	240.00	120.00	60.00
Preliminary examination fee - U.S. was the ISA	600.00	300.00	150.00
Preliminary examination fee - U.S. was not the ISA	760.00	380.00	190.00
Supplemental examination fee per additional invention	600.00	300.00	150.00
Late payment fee	variable	variable	variable
Late furnishing fee for providing a sequence listing in response to an invitation under PCT rule 13*ter*	300.00	150.00	75.00

For more details check
https://www.uspto.gov/patents-getting-started/international-protection/patent-cooperation-treaty/pct-fees-us-dollars

5. After Grant of patent and proceedings

Grant of patent and proceedings

- Grant of patent
- Patent infringement
- What rights you can practice on grant of patent
- Different strategies to monetize your patent

Rights of a patentee

> The grant of patent confers "the right to exclude others from making, using, offering for sale, or selling the invention throughout the United States or importing the invention into the United States" the term of the patent shall be generally 20 years from the date on which the application for the patent was filed in the United States.
>
> It is important to note that, it is the "right to exclude" The patent **does not** grant the right to make, use, offer for sale or sell or import the invention but only grants the exclusive nature of the right.

The patent is issued in the name of the United States under the seal of the United States Patent and Trademark Office, and is either signed by the Director of the USPTO or is electronically written thereon and attested by an Office official. The patent contains a grant to the patentee, and a printed copy of the specification and drawing is annexed to the patent and forms a part of it.

The patent only grants the right to exclude others from making, using, offering for sale or selling or importing the invention. Since the patent does not grant the right to make, use, offer for sale, or sell, or import the invention, the patentee's own right to do so is dependent upon the rights of others and whatever general laws might be applicable.

Generally nothing stops you from making, using, offering for sale, or selling, or importing your own invention, unless you are NOT infringing another's patent that is still in force and / or you are not breaking any law by practicing your invention. In other words, if someone own a patent which you would be infringing if you practice your own invention then that patent owner may prevent you from utilizing your invention.

Patent Infringement

When someone takes actions that infringes on right of patentee then it would be called as patent infringement. Such infringing actions would be the unauthorized making, using, offering for sale, or selling any patented invention within the United States or U.S. Territories, or importing into the United States of any patented invention during the term of the patent.

As per 35 U.S.C. 281 a patentee shall have remedy by civil action for infringement of his patent. If a patent is infringed, the patentee may sue for relief in the appropriate federal court.

- The patentee may ask the court for **an injunction** to prevent the continuation of the infringement and
- may also ask the court for an **award of damages** because of the infringement.

However in such case, the infringing party may want to prove that our patent is **not valid** in the first place, they would be performing invalidity search and would look for ways to make our patent invalid.

The party may also try to prove that his actions does not infringe on your patent.

So, whether the actions from the infringing party would constitute and infringement or not is decided by the claims of your patent. the scope of invention and the acts of infringement are determined by the language of the claims of your patent.

This is why our earlier discussion about writing a patent application such that it would not only survive the examination stage but also it should survive litigation stage is so crucial.

If everything comes down to how well your claim stands in such infringement suits, then protection of the invention by writing most appropriate claims that would provide you the broadest possible protection for your invention becomes such an important thing in the entire lifecycle of a patent that it is make or break deal.

Hence, the importance of going with experienced patent attorney or agent while writing your patent application and especially for writing the claims that would stand through infringement suits by providing the broadest possible protection to your invention.

Another important thing to remember is if you are selling your patented products it is important to mention word "patent" and the number of your patent, because the party who is infringing should be known with the fact that you own the patent rights for the invention and he should be sent a notice if he found to be infringing, if he still continues the infringing acts then you may ask to recover damages.

If the "patent" word and patent number is not mentioned on the product that is patented and the notice is not sent to infringing party then you may not be able to recover the damages.

Let's assume you own a patent for an invention with let's say very high market value. You can call you patent has been infringed, When someone making, using, selling, offering for sale or importing the patented invention without your permission (consent). Permission may typically be granted in the form of a license.

In such scenario you a patent owner can sue the infringing party in federal court. And if you can prove the patent has been infringed, the court can order the infringing party to pay the monetary damages and or stop infringement. This is rewarding if you are a patent owner.

If you happened to be on the other side of the infringement, that is if you are the one who is infringing on someone else's patent, you have an opportunity to prove in the court that the claims of the patent are not valid based on prior arts. For this you need to find prior arts that can convince the court that the claimed invention is indeed known to public and hence cannot be held valid.

This type of search is performed by patent professionals and attorneys called as "validity search" The aim here would be finding prior arts for the independent claims of the given patent so as to prove claims invalid.

Remedy for infringement:

As per 35 U.S.C. 281 If a patent is infringed, the patentee may sue for relief in the appropriate federal court.

Generally the options for remedy are as mentioned below :

- **an injunction** to prevent the continuation of the infringement
- an **award of damages** because of the infringement

strategies to monetize your patent

This is the moment that makes:
- all of efforts you took in research and development,
- filing patent for your invention and
- ultimately getting patent granted for your invention worthwhile.

Now comes the golden time, to get paid for your efforts. As discussed earlier there are different ways to make money from your patented invention.

Licensing your patent to a business:

This is the way preferred by most inventor who comes from technical background and who are also owner of the patent, in this option you license your patented invention to an existing business for whom your invention would be profitable venture and after every sale made or after a fixed time interval you would be **paid royalties** for your patent.

This is most passive form of monetary benefits your would be receiving for your patent. If the company to whom you licensed your patent is significantly large and covers a wider market reach with its products or services, then after each sale (although a fraction of the cost of product) the **money made by you would spectacular** if not significant.

The terms of payment and the percentage sharing would be decided on common agreement between you (patentee) and the company (licensee)

The approach for searching for such a business for licensing is

- doing research and coming up with a list of companies who work in the field of your invention then
- scheduling a meeting with the decision makers and
- presenting them the plan about how this patented invention can be a good fit in their business and they can see significant growth in profits

the most exciting part of this deal would be the **monopoly** you and your licensee going to enjoy for your patented invention !!!

in other words, "when a business sees that licensing patented invention from you would be profitable and more over the competitors cannot compete with this product or service as it is patented... then companies would be more than willing to work with you almost every time"

Another option would be, **Selling your patented invention to a business**

Most of the things discussed in licensing option are applicable here too, the difference being the payment option. Instead of paying on monthly basis or paying royalties behind every sale the company would be more keen to buyout the patent rights from you **at significant one time price.**

In such case the money offered upfront to sell the patent rights could be significant and it would be your decision whether to negotiate further or accept the offer and sell all rights to the company.

Getting funding for your invention

If you have a patent protecting your invention then investors would be more keen to listen to you, and most probably would decide to invest with you. The reason being they speculate that if the product is successful, the competitors would not be able to compete as it is protected with patent, and hence there would be fair chance that investors would make good return on their investment along with your growth.

building business around it

Another very popular way of making money with your patented invention is building business around patented invention. Or may be protecting your existing business and invention by means of patents from competition.

This path is most rewarding and most travelled by entrepreneurs and business owners... and it is more promising as well as you are in complete control and the amount of money you are going to make is not dependent on an agreement with other party or how well other party does the business after licensing..

On the other hand there are many entrepreneurs who happen to found an innovative idea while working on some problems go for patent and end up making large sums of money by leveraging patent protection.

And not to forget you can make money in one more way that is filing a suit of infringement and if it is proven in the court you would be rewarded with reliefs.

All this is applicable if your patented invention has commercial value in the market. That is the main essence of all this monetizing strategies.

The patents are as valuable as they are worth in commercial use. In other words, there has to be a commercial value for the invention that you are patenting, there need to be companies, businesses who would potentially want to use your invention and paying you royalties. Or companies who could be interested in buying out your patent if you are willing to sale it.

If this part is missing, that is your invention is does not have any commercial value then probably your patent for that invention would also be worthless.

The amount of money to be made by patenting your invention completely depends on how much commercially valuable your invention is, and your ability to commercially exploit your patented invention.

6. What how why when: Answers to important questions

What how why when: Answers to important questions

- Cost of getting patent in US (a short note)
- How to hire right patent attorney in US: steps and selection criteria's
- Most expensive v/s most economic patent practitioner
- How much time required ?
- When is the right time to file a patent application
- Patent Pending status and its advantages
- I am in research and development is patent relevant for me?
- Not patentable? Here is another option for protection
- Advantages of trade secret
- Combining trademark and trade secret protection

What is cost of getting patent in US ?

How much is the cost of getting patent in US ? There is no precise and accurate answer to this question as cost for obtaining patent is dependent on multiple factors...

There are two elements for cost of getting patent in US:

- USPTO fees for filing, search, and examination etc.
- Professional Charges for patent practitioner (patent agent / attorney)

let's see these fees and charges involved in getting patent in US in step by step, detailed and easy to understand manner as below:

As a matter of fact Patent attorney Professional charges is the most expensive component which drastically varies based on complexity of the invention to be patented, field of invention and the experience of the patent attorney.

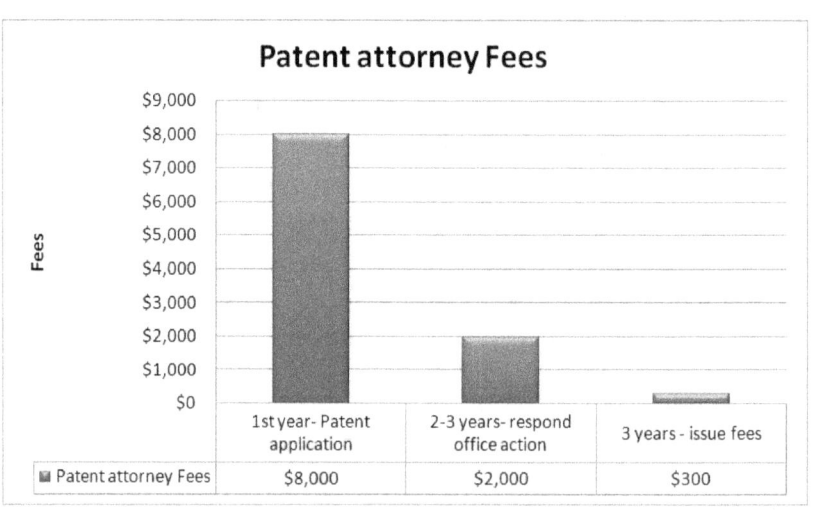

USPTO fees are different for micro entities, small entities and regular applicant. Also it depends on number of claims and sheets in patent application

So, a **lot of factors need to be considered** when talking about costs involved in getting patent in US.

Lets briefly go through stage wise approximate costs for getting patent in US.

- Novelty Search (about $ 2000),
- Patent drafting and filing in US (about $8,000) and
- for responding to office actions, if any (about $1000)

Note: these costs are mentioned are exemplary and may vary with respect to patent attorneys / agents.

Stage 1: invention disclosure

The comprehensive invention disclosure is the outcome of the idea incubation phase (separate chapter in this book). This is initial phase when you (inventor) disclose your invention to the patent attorney you selected to work with by signing a Non disclosure agreement. This agreement is to ensure the confidentiality of your invention and there are no charges for signing NDA.

When writing Invention disclosure for your invention you, do a complete research and should submit each know fact about your invention, description diagrams and experimental results (if any). Hold nothing back. The disclosure of the invention must be:

- described in substantial details
- includes picture, flowcharts, diagrams where ever applicable
- Optionally includes experimental data proving novelty and non obviousness
- Charts and tables about research and development

This helps patent attorney in patent research as well as drafting process.

Stage 2: Novelty search / Patentability search

Simple invention	Complex invention	Very complex invention
$500	$1500	$2500

In this phase, patent professional performed an extensive search for prior art in all possible databases for patent, articles, thesis etc... And builds a patentability search report based on closest prior art found for your invention.

Although **an optional step**, Doing novelty search for your invention can really save you thousands of dollars for involving in patent process for an invention which is not novel and already known to public.

Stage 3: Opinion about patentability

Upon receiving the novelty search report (from the researcher appointed) it is critically reviewed by patent attorney to build an opinion about patentability of your invention. As discussed in detailed in chapter "working with patent agent or attorney" the patentability opinion could be negative, neutral or positive depending upon the results obtained in search report.

Here the cost defers based on complexity of invention and number of closely associated prior arts found in the research. This opinion tells you (inventor or applicant) whether the invention would be patentable and whether your should proceed with patent filing process.

Cost: the cost for providing patentability opinion ranges from $200 to $1000

Stage 4: Patent writing or patent drafting

drafting Provisional Patent application in US:

Simple invention	Complex invention	Very complex invention
$2000	$3000	$5000

drafting Non-Provisional (complete) Patent application in US:

Simple invention	Complex invention	Very complex invention
$5000	$8000	$10000

Time : it takes about 1 to 2 weeks time for patent attorney to draft an application for an invention. It certainly can take more time based on complexity, length of detailed description and availability of patent attorney's time.

Stage 5: Filing Patent application

filing fees for Provisional application in US

Large entity	Small entity	Micro entity
$280	$140	$70

Non provisional Patent application

Basic filing fee - Utility (paper filing also requires non-electronic filing fee under 1.16(t))

Large entity	Small entity	Micro entity
$300	$150	$75

When you done with the review of patent drafted and satisfied with the scope and technical details in the patent application, you should file the patent application at USPTO soon as possible.

Stage 6: Publication of patent application occurs after the expiration of an 18-month period following the earliest effective filing date or priority date claimed by an application.

Stage 7: Patent Examination

Patent Examination Fees

Description	Fee	Small Entity Fee	Micro Entity Fee
Utility Examination Fee	760.00	380.00	190.00

After the application is filed, the U. S. Patent Office takes the application up for examination (usually in about 12-36 months). In this stage patent examiners at USPTO conduct their own search related to your invention (patent application) and issue and office action.

Stage 8: Office action

Cost : The patent practitioner (attorney / agent) charges anything from $500 to $1500 for response to office action.

Office action contains the objections raised about your patent application by patent examiner, which can range from variety of objections. You (inventor) has a chance to respond to objection and put your side in-front of examiner, this is something called "response to office actions" in most of the cases the response is drafted with the help of your patent attorney.

Stage 9: Issue of Patent

Description	Fee	Small Entity Fee	Micro Entity Fee
Utility issue fee	1,000.00	500.00	250.00

The patent is granted to you (inventor) if it is found to be meeting all patentability requirements !!! or it may be rejected if it happen to be not meeting patentability criteria's.

If a patent application is found to be in order of grant a Notice of Allowance and Fee(s) Due will be sent to the applicant, or to applicant's patent attorney. a fee for issuing the patent and if applicable, for publishing the patent application publication.

Stage 10: Renewal of patent fees

Once the patent is granted, it will be valid for up to 20 years from the date of filing the application. Inventor required to pay a maintenance fees periodically (as mentioned below) to maintain patent in force.

Patent Maintenance Fees

Description	Fee	Small Entity Fee	Micro Entity Fee
For maintaining an original or any reissue patent, due at 3.5 years	1,600.00	800.00	400.00
For maintaining an original or any reissue patent, due at 7.5 years	3,600.00	1,800.00	900.00
For maintaining an original or any reissue patent, due at 11.5 years	7,400.00	3,700.00	1,850.00

How to hire right patent attorney in US : steps and selection criteria's

If you are still confused whether you would end up saving few thousands of dollars by writing and filing your patent application on your own (without help of patent attorney) you can read section in this book on "do I really need a patent agent / attorney ?"

Now the next question is;

Out of thousands if not hundreds of patent practitioners in US, How would I find the right one for my invention ? and importantly at right costs ???

Selection process for right patent attorney could turn out more complex process than you would initially imagine. Even though Google search is there to help with your decision making, yet as they say "all shining objects are not gold"

You may find most websites sound similar and it is quite difficult to differentiate patent attorney with regards to superior quality.

This problem is more intense for first time inventors (who have not filed the patent before) who are searching for a good patent attorney and **not specifically knowing what to look for** when selecting right patent attorney for protecting their invention in US.

Selecting a right patent attorney is significantly expensive decision that you are going to make and you would not want to be making mistakes in it.

"A patent attorney charges anything from $200 to $500 per hour"

Hence it is wise to be prepared. As you might have guessed, Good reputation and experience in dealing with patents from field of your invention is primary short listing factor and you can get to a shortlisted list of patent attorneys:

Does patent Attorney have degree in your field of invention?

This is not always required, as patent practitioners are known to work in many fields but still it would help if their degree is match with the field of your invention, for obvious reasons like familiarity with the subject matter of the invention.

Personal visit to patent attorney's office:
Ideally it is recommended to visit shortlisted patent attorneys as a primary meeting and get a sense of proceedings by meeting one on one; there are far too many advantages to in person meeting before selecting a professional. It's just way comprehensive than discussing on email or a call.

Short listing calls to attorneys:
If the list of shortlisted patent attorneys is longer and you are unable to distinguish between them with the help of their online profiles It's better to further shortlist them by scheduling a short phone call (5 to 10 minutes) with the patent attorney who is going to work on your invention.

The some of the things to discuss in call or meeting would be:
- systems or process they follow for taking new client invention disclosure to granted patent
- cost estimate for proceeding with your patent requirement
- what in included and what is not included in the cost estimate shared
- Ask for previous work (granted patents) in same field of your invention:
- The previous work reveals too many things about quality of research and drafting for patents on which the attorney already worked on, like
- granted patents
- novelty search reports and
- responses to office actions
- any other relevant work samples from your field of invention

You can visualize your end results comparing to previous work shared by the patent attorneys in communication.

Honestly disclosing real results for novelty search:
This is another factor needed to be considered as in some cases the novelty search for the invention disclosure provided is not performed with adequate quality and attention to ensure positive opinion of patentability... so that a client (applicant) moves ahead with drafting and filing of the patent application.

Although this unethical practice is rare, it is however best avoided if patent attorney appoints an independent patent research expert for performing novelty search and provides honest patentability opinion.

How is your comfort level when communicating with patent attorney?

This is to be decided on more of a gut feeling but nevertheless this is still important factor in selecting right patent attorney to work on your invention. An in person first visit with patent attorney / agent really helps in coming conclusion with this question.

Have your own thoughts and opinion and trust on your gut feeling as once selected, you are likely to work with him for years to come, even after grant of patent.

Now regarding making decision based on Patent attorney charges, below is the most common question in minds of inventor

Shall I go for most expensive patent attorney or most economic one?

Cost for getting patent for your invention in US heavily depends on the attorney you choose to work with.

Patent practitioner (agent or attorney) helps you in preparing a patent application which will provide broadest possible protection to your invention and which will stand through examination phase, office actions, litigation phase and ultimately monetization phase.

Hence it is the decision having significant importance!!!

Patent attorneys charges typically vary with their **expertise and experience**, highly experienced patent professional charge the highest amounts, and you probably do not need the highest possible patent professional in US to work on your invention as it could be super expensive.

Having said that, **you also don't want to be working with really inexperienced patent attorney who is just starting out or who will charge ridiculously low fees compared to other patent attorneys.**

In such cases you are at the risk of losing entire efforts you put in research and development along with the rights on your invention if it is not well written and not protected with appropriate claims...

"Ideal case would be patent attorney with **moderate charges and significant experience in your field of invention** who can give justice to your efforts and protect your invention to fullest possible extent."

If you happened to make a mistake, be sure that you are selecting higher side of the costing... rather than selecting an attorney with lowest possible charges...

This is because, **you still will be on winning side** even if you choose slightly highly charged patent attorney as he will ensure that your invention would be appropriately protected !!! and you do not end up losing rights on your invention due to poor quality of patent application. Or end up with granted patent which has claims that do not provide adequate protection to your invention and hence fail to monetize the patent.

How much time required ?

How much time will it take for my invention to get patent in US? When you (inventor) ask about time required to get patent in US for my invention, even if did not specifically mentioned, there are 2 intentions behind asking that question and ultimately 2 answers:

1. Time required to file patent in US for your invention
2. Time required to get Granted patent in US for your invention

A quick answer to 1st point is: It takes about 2-3 weeks for a patent attorney to write patent application and file it. Steps include
- novelty search
- patentability opinion
- drafting patent application and
- filing patent application at USPTO

And the quick answer to 2nd point is: generally, It takes about 2-3 years to get granted patent in US for your invention. However there are ways to speed up the process and reduce this time discussed in this book.

Steps for grant include
- Publication of application
- Examination
- Examination report
- Office action
- Grant of patent

you can read section on "patent basics, procedure and costs "for getting patent in US

When a typical inventor gets to know that it takes more than 2 years to get granted patent for his invention, His immediate questions in minds would be; Do I have to wait for 2-3 years to do anything about my invention? Till the patent is granted? How it will make sense in my current business to wait for such long time period? Should I really go for patenting?

The most important fact to consider here is; You get the status of "patent pending" in US as soon as you file the patent application. (that is in 1-2 weeks time as per above mentioned point 1) You (inventor) do not need to wait till grant of patent for most of the activities (95% of them) like:

- Talking to investors and financers to get funding
- Researching the financial worth of the invention
- Finding right partners for building business around invention
- Advertising and commercializing
- Practicing the invention for trail purpose with some clients
- Searching for right partner to license the patent after granted
- Or in some cases entirely selling the invention as patent pending

However, The only thing **you cannot do** till you have granted patent on your name for the invention is "stop others from practicing invention for commercial purpose"!!!

In other words, you cannot stop others from using, selling, offering for sale or importing your invention until and unless you have granted patent on your name for the invention.

almost all other activities (even selling of the patent in process) can be done after you have filled the patent application that is your invention is having "patent pending" status.

Hence even if it takes more than 2 years to get granted patent for your invention, It doesn't stop you from doing almost all activities generally related to patent as soon as you file the patent !!!

When is the right time to file a patent application

Ideally the time to file patent application is as soon as possible there are few reasons to consider:

- US follows first to file approach for patent system
- to secure the priority date for patent application as early as possible filing patent application as early as possible helps in minimizing the possibility of prior arts, since more time you will take to file patent application chances are that would be more and more possible prior arts available to public.
- if you significantly delay the patent filing process even your own work could become a prior art and hence can stop you from getting your invention patented (although there is 1 year grace period in US that you can leverage)
- if you are working on invention which has very heavy competition and many players in the market are doing research and development in the same field, then you should file patent application as soon as possible.

Patent Pending or Patent applied status and its advantages

You can write "patent pending" status in front of your technology / product as soon as you filed the patent application in USPTO. It may be provisional or complete patent application.

There are some subtle advantages of writing patent pending next to name of your product of service.

- This gives an immediate impression of superior product or technology in minds of reader
- Seeing the patent pending or patent applied for status many of the competitors would be discouraged anticipating they would not be able to compete in same domain if you got granted patent
- This sends a message to public that the patent has been applied for this innovative technology

- You investors and financers take you more seriously if you have patent pending status

Having said this, there is no legal significance of these words. The infringement suit can be initiated only after the patent is granted.

I am in research and development how patent relevant for me?

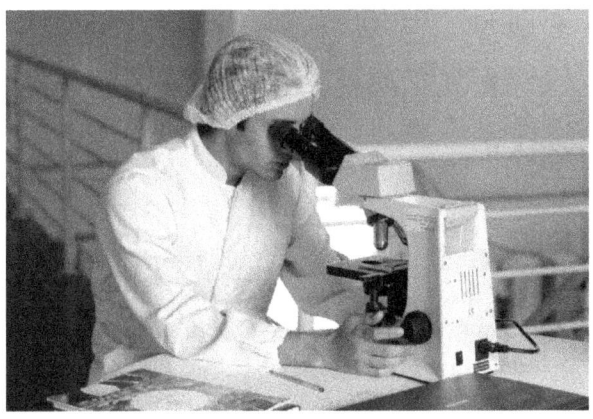

As a research and development person, you need to be very careful that you are not putting all of your efforts in something which is already invented and patented. If that becomes the case, you would be **re-inventing wheel** and probably all your research efforts are not going to be worth whole a lot.

Having said that, we have also seen many people working on particular invention getting discouraged up on finding hundreds and thousands of patent from their domain and similar to their technology. This could also be a mistake.

We have a section in this book for when to get encouraged and when to get discouraged base on the results of the preliminary search conducted in chapter "Idea incubation phase"

Getting patent for an invention does not always requires and invention to be something earth breaking solution, but many patents are awarded for incremental inventions too, that means most of the part of the invention would already be known to public but a small (but significant) part which is called as **'inventive feature'** is the novel and non obvious part that could win patent for your invention.

So, a prior art documents or patents that are already existing can be 95% similar to your invention Yet, if your invention has either technical advance or economic significance or both... and you can prove it that your invention is better than existing ones then there is a strong possibility that you may get patent for your invention.

The best way to take this judgment is get help from Patent practitioner, The novelty search (also called as patentability search) is performed for the same reason, this patentability search, done right, can yield pretty fantastic results for your invention;

- It can tell you what part of your invention is already covered and what could be novel and non obvious feature
- it can tell you where you can focus you research work to get maximum level of protection with you patent
- and it gives a review about whether it is appropriate to proceed with patent filing process

http://patentattorneyworldwide.com/us/

Not patentable? Here is another option for protection

Reference:
http://www.wipo.int/sme/en/ip_business/trade_secrets/patent_trade.htm

what if your innovative idea is found to be **non patentable** ?? There is another way you can protect your innovative idea from competition and that way is trade secret.

however this is not necessarily for ideas or innovations that are non patentable but even patentable invention can also be protected as trade secrets.

A trade secret is a formula, practice, process, design, instrument, pattern, commercial method, or compilation of information not generally known or reasonably ascertainable by others by which a business can obtain an economic advantage over competitors or customers.

- It is secret
- It confers a competitive advantage on its owner
- It is subject to reasonable efforts to maintain its secrecy

The first thing is **the information should be secret**, that is it should not be readily available to competitors or is generally known by public.

In our example of Coca Cola if one of the competitor beverages manufacturing company figure out the formula for Coca Cola then it would lose its secret status although it is not available to the public at large.

The second important thing is the **information should have some competitive advantage** how economic advantage to the corner of the trade secret.

And third point is the owner of trade secret should take **reasonable efforts to keep the information secret** and not disclose it in the public domain

Trade secrets for a business can range from specific formula or manufacturing process to a list of clients.

An example of a trade secret would be the formula and composition of materials used to create the Coca-Cola. unlike patents you don't need to disclose the entire innovative idea to get the trade secret...

advantages of using trade secret

So if you are thinking about protecting your innovative ideas with trade secret following are the advantages of using trade secret:

- The biggest advantage is it doesn't require any registration cost
- and unlike patent they are not Limited for 20 years of time that is the protection is valid as long as the secret is not reveal to the public
- trade secret does not require any formalities or disclosure of innovative ideas to government authorities
- and like patents trade secret does not require waiting period like for grant of patent.
- And trade secret costs must less when compared to Cost of filing patent in US
- Trade secrets do not require public disclosure, and aren't subject to the same formal application process or expense.

In general the cost of maintaining confidentiality and protecting trade secrets is internal costs of administration and install inappropriate procedures in the business.

I am sure you would be impressed by the simplicity and ease of protection provided by trade secrets, Particularly the idea that you don't need to disclose your business secret or innovative idea to anyone else and no formalities required;

what can go wrong? you have complete control on your inventive idea for business secret. to understand this

let's take an exemplary scenario:

Let's say you have come up with an inventive product A. which is found to be patentable and you are considering whether you should protect it by means of patents or by means of trade secrets...

if you choose to go by trade secret and reject the options for getting patent, there are few things that could go wrong:

When you produce your inventive product A, and commercially sell in the market, and it is really successful, probability is competitors would be watching it and they will analyze and **reverse engineer your product** A and will figure out your invention (that is your trade secret in this case) and when this happens unlike patents; **trade secret does not give your right to exclude others** from commercially utilizing your invention,

so in a way the protection provided by trade secret in terms of excluding competition from using your innovative idea is weaker than patent. The only protection for trade secrets is on the grounds of **misappropriation** of trade secrets.

The very simplicity and informal nature of protection that we are impressed by earlier is in fact becomes a difficulty when we try to enforce trade secrets by misappropriation:

- in this case you have to prove that the person who has acquired the trade secrets from you is by improper way...
- Generally this becomes a week case and since there are no formal documentation available or government parties involved like in case of patents,
- in most of the cases it is difficult to prove with ambiguous claims.
- And if we cannot prove that then the other person can legally use our trade secret....

And that is why the **patent is such a big winner !!!** and most favorite means of protection of innovative ideas for entrepreneurs and business owners.

Although trade secret seems easier to protect your innovative ideas in reality it is difficult and costly to protect your business secret and it is even difficult to enforce when compared with patent.

and if you have an option to select that is if the innovative idea in consideration is eligible to get patent for it **you should consider patenting it in most of the cases.**

Having said this even trade secrets are potent for of protection for your innovative ideas and business Secrets.

Combining trademark and trade secret protection

So if you combine trade secret protection with a trademark protection of your innovative ideas, in certain cases it becomes comparable protection with patents !!!

In a famous example of "Coca-Cola" the brand is protected by trademark and the secret ingredients, recipe and process to create the famous beverage is a well kept secret since decades, that is achieved by trade secrets !!!

and if you have observe the evaluation of intellectual property (trademarks and trade secrets) of companies like coca cola is way greater than the physical assets of the company (like machineries, factories etc...)

"So.. in essence, trademark and trade secret protections combined together may provide a very strong protection for your intellectual property."

In recent case with best buy they have finalized for 27 million dollars in one of the case for in a preparation of trade secret from a small startup company. the link is provided below

http://www.startribune.com/best-buy-to-pay-27-million-in-trade-secrets-case/182365221/

Now let's see some of the examples what information in your business can be trade secret:

- Any information that is created by our business in order to perform its functions Efficiently
- The process and methods used in business operation
- List of clients, original equipment manufacturers, suppliers
- pricing strategy and profit margins
- growth strategies Business plans or business development strategies

- wisdom gain by business from field experiments
- know how about some important functions
- research and development conducted
- Technical details and specifications of product
- software or hardware involved in certain processes
- chemical composition and formula etc...

sometimes identifying the trade secret is not that obvious and you need to drill down by asking you questions about your business like,

"what is the most important information in my business if it is found out by others I will lose the competitive advantage of my business ?"

Where are the steps for protecting your business Secret by means of trade secret:

Find out what really is important information for your business need to be kept secret And create a document mentioning the trade secrets for the business.

Keeping It confidential: You need to take appropriate care for maintaining confidentiality of this information for example: if your secret is in computer the access should be Limited to only authorized users, and information should not be available publicly. and if the trade secret is in the physical document format. should be kept in safe area and location where the unauthorized access is restricted

Non disclosure and non compete agreement:

As a part of general practice to maintain confidentiality of the important information of the business, all the employees of your business should be signing non disclosure and non compete agreements.

perform regular audits about the confidentiality of ongoing business information and make employees aware about maintaining secrecy of the information time to time.

Trade Secrets Law Prohibits "Misappropriation" of Trade Secrets

Section 1(2) of the UTSA provides the following definition for the term:

"Misappropriation " means:
- acquisition of a trade secret of another by a person who knows or has reason to know that the trade secret was acquired by improper means; or
- disclosure or use of a trade secret of another without express or implied consent by a person who
    - used improper means to acquire knowledge of the trade secret; or
    - at the time of disclosure or use knew or had reason to know that his knowledge of the trade secret was
- derived from or through a person who has utilized improper means to acquire it;
- acquired under circumstances giving rise to a duty to maintain its secrecy or limit its use; or
- derived from or through a person who owed a duty to the person seeking relief to maintain its secrecy or limit its use; or
    - before a material change of his position, knew or had reason to know that it was a trade secret ad that knowledge of it had been acquired by accident or mistake.

following things will come under misappropriation of trade secrets:

If you obtain trade Secret by improper means which includes theft, fraud, bribery, breaching a contractual duty to keep something confidential, or inducing others to breach that duty.

An example of situation would be if one of your employees taking the confidential information from your business to his home which is violating the confidentiality agreement or if an employee makes illegal copies of confidential information from your computer.

If you make the trade secret public which was required by other person that you know is by improper means...

Or if one of your employee have done confidentiality agreement with previous company and he is disclosing the secret information to you knowing that he already have signed the non disclosure agreement would also breach the agreement.

Having said this,

If one of your competitor **reverse engineer your product** or services and **figure out on his own** the trade secret information then this does not come under improper means of obtaining information. Hence this cannot be claimed as misappropriation !!!

and this is probably the biggest **loophole or disadvantages** of trade secret when we compare it with patents. You cannot protect your business against the legal discovery of your trade Secrets by your competitors. that is why, when compared to patents, trade secrets are considered weaker form of protection !!!

However you can further strengthen the confidentiality of the trade secret by making a contract with your clients and customers to agree **not to reverse engineer the product** in the form of end-user licensing agreement

Choosing between trade secret and patents

This selection depends on how we are going to use the innovative idea or the information to be protected.

for example if your invention is something that will become obvious when it is released as a product and very easy to reverse engineer then the best way to approach this is by patents.

on the other hand if the invention is secret information that is **not easy to reverse engineer** like a recipe for food product then it is best protected by trade secret. because if it gets published there is possibility and threat of competitors using it by changing few elements of the patented invention without in fencing on your patent.

this is called "work around". That is Practicing the invention without infringing on the claims of our patent.

And it is better to take advice from an experienced Patent attorney who would help in taking right decisions for your business !!!

7. Important tables charts and references

Code	Rule	Description	Fee	Small	Micro
1081/2081/3081	1.16(s)	Utility Application Size Fee - for each additional 50 sheets that exceeds 100 sheets	400.00	200.00	100.00
1082/2082/3082	1.16(s)	Design Application Size Fee - for each additional 50 sheets that exceeds 100 sheets	400.00	200.00	100.00
1083/2083/3083	1.16(s)	Plant Application Size Fee - for each additional 50 sheets that exceeds 100 sheets	400.00	200.00	100.00
1084/2084/3084	1.16(s)	Reissue Application Size Fee - for each additional 50 sheets that exceeds 100 sheets	400.00	200.00	100.00
1085/2085/3085	1.16(s)	Provisional Application Size Fee - for each additional 50 sheets that exceeds 100 sheets	400.00	200.00	100.00
1090/2090/3090	1.16(t)	Non-electronic filing fee — Utility (additional fee for applications filed in paper)	400.00	200.00	200.00
1053/2053/3053	1.17(i)(1)	Non-English translation	140.00	70.00	35.00
1091/2091/3091	1.21(o)(1)	Submission of sequence listings of 300MB to 800MB	1,000.00	500.00	250.00
1092/2092/3092	1.21(o)(2)	Submission of sequence listings of more than 800MB	10,000.00	5,000.00	2,500.00
† The 4000 series fee code may be used via EFS-Web					
		least one claim or by reference			
1052/2052/3052	1.16(g)	Surcharge - Late provisional filing fee or cover sheet	60.00	30.00	15.00
1201/2201/3201	1.16(h)	Each independent claim in excess of three	460.00	230.00	115.00
1204/2204/3204	1.16(h)	Each reissue independent claim in excess of three	460.00	230.00	115.00
1202/2202/3202	1.16(i)	Each claim in excess of 20	100.00	50.00	25.00
1205/2205/3205	1.16(i)	Each reissue claim in excess of 20	100.00	50.00	25.00
1203/2203/3203	1.16(j)	Multiple dependent claim	820.00	410.00	205.00

http://patentattorneyworldwide.com/us/

Patent Search Fees					
Fee Code	37 CFR	Description	Fee	Small Entity Fee	Micro Entity Fee
1111/2111/3111	1.16(k)	Utility Search Fee	660.00	330.00	165.00
1112/2112/3112	1.16(l)	Design Search Fee or Design CPA Search Fee	160.00	80.00	40.00
1113/2113/3113	1.16(m)	Plant Search Fee	420.00	210.00	105.00
1114/2114/3114	1.16(n)	Reissue Search Fee or Reissue (Design CPA) Search Fee	660.00	330.00	165.00

Patent Examination Fees					
Fee Code	37 CFR	Description	Fee	Small Entity Fee	Micro Entity Fee
1311/2311/3311	1.16(o)	Utility Examination Fee	760.00	380.00	190.00
1312/2312/3312	1.16(p)	Design Examination Fee or Design CPA Examination Fee	600.00	300.00	150.00
1313/2313/3313	1.16(q)	Plant Examination Fee	620.00	310.00	155.00
1314/2314/3314	1.16(r)	Reissue Examination Fee or Reissue (Design CPA) Examination Fee	2,200.00	1,100.00	550.00

Patent Post-Allowance Fees					
Fee Code	37 CFR	Description	Fee	Small Entity Fee	Micro Entity Fee
1501/2501/3501	1.18(a)(1)	Utility issue fee	1,000.00	500.00	250.00
1511/2511/3511	1.18(a)(1)	Reissue issue fee	1,000.00	500.00	250.00
1502/2502/3502	1.18(b)(1)	Design issue fee	700.00	350.00	175.00
1503/2503/3503	1.18(c)(1)	Plant issue fee	800.00	400.00	200.00
n/a	1.18(d)(1)	Publication fee for early, voluntary, or normal publication	0.00	0.00	0.00
1505/2505/3505	1.18(d)(3)	Publication fee for republication	300.00	300.00	300.00*

* Third-party filers are not eligible for the micro entity fee.

Patent Maintenance Fees					
Fee Code	37 CFR	Description	Fee	Small Entity Fee	Micro Entity Fee
1551/2551/3551	1.20(e)	For maintaining an original or any reissue patent, due at 3.5 years	1,600.00	800.00	400.00
1552/2552/3552	1.20(f)	For maintaining an original or any reissue patent, due at 7.5 years	3,600.00	1,800.00	900.00
1553/2553/3553	1.20(g)	For maintaining an original or any reissue patent, due at 11.5 years	7,400.00	3,700.00	1,850.00
1554/2554/3554	1.20(h)	Surcharge - 3.5 year - Late payment within 6 months	160.00	80.00	40.00
1555/2555/3555	1.20(h)	Surcharge - 7.5 year - Late payment within 6 months	160.00	80.00	40.00
1556/2556/3556	1.20(h)	Surcharge - 11.5 year - Late payment within 6 months	160.00	80.00	40.00
1558/2558/3558	1.17(m)	Petition for the delayed payment of the fee for maintaining a patent in force	2,000.00	1,000.00	500.00

www.ingramcontent.com/pod-product-compliance
Lightning Source LLC
Chambersburg PA
CBHW052322220526
45472CB00001B/229